The Food Allergy Mama's
Easy, Fast Family Meals

KELLY RUDNICKI

The Food Allergy Mama's Easy, Fast Family Meals

Dairy, Egg, and Nut Free Recipes
for Every Day

AVERY
a member of Penguin Group (USA) Inc.
New York

AVERY

Published by the Penguin Group

Penguin Group (USA) Inc., 375 Hudson Street, New York, New York 10014, USA • Penguin Group (Canada), 90 Eglinton Avenue East,
Suite 700, Toronto, Ontario M4P 2Y3, Canada (a division of Pearson Penguin Canada Inc.) • Penguin Books Ltd, 80 Strand, London WC2R 0RL, England •
Penguin Ireland, 25 St Stephen's Green, Dublin 2, Ireland (a division of Penguin Books Ltd) • Penguin Group (Australia), 707 Collins Street, Melbourne, Victoria 3008,
Australia (a division of Pearson Australia Group Pty Ltd) • Penguin Books India Pvt Ltd, 11 Community Centre, Panchsheel Park, New Delhi–110 017, India •
Penguin Group (NZ), 67 Apollo Drive, Rosedale, Auckland 0632, New Zealand (a division of Pearson New Zealand Ltd) • Penguin Books (South Africa),
Rosebank Office Park, 181 Jan Smuts Avenue, Parktown North 2193, South Africa • Penguin China, B7 Jiaming Center,
27 East Third Ring Road North, Chaoyang District, Beijing 100020, China

Penguin Books Ltd, Registered Offices: 80 Strand, London WC2R 0RL, England

Most Avery books are available at special quantity discounts for bulk purchase for sales promotions, premiums,
fund-raising, and educational needs. Special books or book excerpts also can be created to fit specific needs.
For details, write Penguin Group (USA) Inc. Special Markets, 375 Hudson Street, New York, NY 10014.

Library of Congress Cataloging-in-Publication Data

Rudnicki, Kelly, date.
The food allergy mama's easy, fast family meals : dairy, egg, and nut free recipes for every day / Kelly Rudnicki.
p.   cm
ISBN 978-1-58333-500-0
1. Food allergy—Diet therapy—Recipes.   2. Quick and easy cooking.   I. Title.
RC588.D53R82   2012   2012039957
641.5'6318—dc23

Printed in the United States of America
1   3   5   7   9   10   8   6   4   2

This book is printed on acid-free paper. ♾

BOOK DESIGN BY TANYA MAIBORODA

Neither the publisher nor the author is engaged in rendering professional advice or services to the individual reader. The ideas, procedures, and suggestions contained in this book are not intended as a substitute for consulting with your physician. All matters regarding your health require medical supervision. Neither the author nor the publisher shall be liable or responsible for any loss or damage allegedly arising from any information or suggestion in this book.

The recipes contained in this book are to be followed exactly as written. The publisher is not responsible for your specific health or allergy needs that may require medical supervision. The publisher is not responsible for any adverse reactions to the recipes contained in this book.

While the author has made every effort to provide accurate telephone numbers, Internet addresses, and other contact information at the time of publication, neither the publisher nor the author assumes any responsibility for errors, or for changes that occur after publication. Further, the publisher does not have any control over and does not assume any responsibility for author or third-party websites or their content.

Contents

Many Thanks

THIS BOOK WAS A TRUE WORK OF LOVE FOR ME. I SPENT A LOT OF TIME in the kitchen with my children creating and testing, then often scrapping the original recipes and trying again. In fact, one of the greatest things my children learned in creating this book is that mistakes sometimes can be a gift, and often bring you to something greater. I think this is true about life in general. If we are able to show our children how imperfect we are and share our willingness to try something new even if it doesn't work out, then we've given them the gift of allowing them to feel like they don't have to be perfect and to embrace their inner creativity. We all have something great to create, whether it's a delicious meal or the special memories behind the meal.

This book was made possible by the love and support of many. My greatest thanks and love go to my husband, Mike, and children, Chloe, John, Matthew, David, and Michael. They are my life's greatest gift, and I'm grateful for their support, patience, and willingness to give up free time with me so I could cook and write. This book never would have been possible without them. Another equally important family member is my sister, Chris, who was always there to throw her love and support and guidance my way. She's the best friend and sister one could ever wish for, and I can't imagine my life without her. And to my other angel, Halina Pieklo, who lovingly cared for all five of my children during my busiest of days, keeping them occupied while keeping me organized. I love you as if you were my own mother, Halina, and hope I can be as great a mother as you someday.

This book also would not be possible without the unlimited support of my agent, Marilyn Allen, who worked tirelessly to get my book into loving hands. Those loving hands, editor extraordinaire Marisa Vigilante and president William Shinker at Avery/Penguin Books, believed in my book with the same passion as I did, and I am tremendously lucky to have some of the most talented people in the publishing world work on my book.

I also owe a gigantic thanks to the amazing Robert Knapp for the beautiful photography in this book. I have yet to work with someone as talented as he, for his photos really capture the story as well as the look and feel of the recipes. I thank Mark Czerniec for always taking care of my technical issues, as I'm so incapable of this myself. A huge thank-you to Natasha Miller for making my dreams possible during one of the busiest times of my life, and helping me every step of the way.

To all my other wonderful family, best girlfriends, dear friends, incredible neighbors, awesome teachers, and everyone else who showed their unwavering love and support, I thank you from the bottom of my heart. Projects like this are only possible with the caring and help of others.

Finally, my biggest thanks go to all the food allergy mamas, dads, grandmas, grandpas, teachers, and friends in the world, who have inspired me through their e-mails and encouraging words of support. *Your* stories of love and dedication for your children's happiness, safety, and well-being made me want to become a better mom, writer, and cook. I am so blessed to have had the opportunity to share this journey with you. Happy cooking *and* happy baking!

About the Book

FAMILIES, NOT JUST THOSE SUFFERING FROM FOOD ALLERGIES, ARE returning to the kitchen table now more than ever. A recent study found that nearly 60 percent of families in America eat supper together at least five times a week, up from 47 percent in 1998. This is especially true for families who have to live with severe food allergies. Families living with food allergies don't have the luxury of eating out or ordering in food. They must cook at home as much as possible in order to keep their food-allergic children safe. But it's also important to emphasize the togetherness of mealtime and make it a wonderful, positive experience. Like everyone else, they just want to enjoy deliciously prepared food, but they don't want to spend a lot of time in the kitchen trying to prepare difficult recipes with hard-to-find ingredients.

My first book, *The Food Allergy Mama's Baking Book,* was written for the food allergy mama looking for delicious, sweet recipes that worked every time. What

I didn't expect were the countless grandparents, neighbors, friends, and teachers who loved my book and who also used it with great success. It was a tremendous honor to create simple yet family-favorite treats that everyone loved, not just those who suffered from food allergies. Over the last several years, I've happily shared my favorite recipes, tips, and personal stories of trials and tribulations on my blog, www.foodallergymama.com. I received so many incredible e-mails and comments from readers around the world, sharing their own successes as well as their heartbreaks. But the one question people kept asking me was, "What do you make your family for lunch and dinner?" I decided it was time to write the book I wished I already had on my own kitchen counter.

The Food Allergy Mama's Easy, Fast Family Meals is my answer to what I love to serve my own family, week in and week out. It's what I know my own picky eaters will eat, as will their friends. I've written this for the food allergy mama who isn't a pro in the kitchen, who doesn't have time to shop in multiple stores for hard-to-find ingredients, and who probably is juggling kids, homework, and carpools in that crazy time known as the "witching hour." This book is for you, because I know what you are up against on a daily basis.

In addition to my food-allergic ten-year-old son, John, I also have a twelve-year-old, seven-year-old, six-year-old, and two-year-old. Four children play sports, one takes music lessons, and another just plays. Our days are full, as I know yours probably are too, so I wrote this book with the daily grind in mind and tried to imagine which recipes could be made simply, easily, and in a relatively short amount of time.

I don't believe in standing by the stovetop, sautéing away the night's supper, because usually my two-year-old is tugging at my leg, wanting something. Or one of the kids is yelling for help with homework. Or perhaps there's a knock on my back door for one of my kids to go out and play some basketball. In other words, I like to use only recipes that are fast, or can be made ahead of time, perhaps when the kids are at school or little ones are napping. Sundays are great days to cook for the week. It's all about time management and efficiency.

You will see a lot of recipes here that build on others that help make the most of leftovers, a food allergy mama's biggest helper. Easy ones like Weekday Double Roast Chicken (page 139) will make at least two meals by using the chicken for other delicious meals like Chicken Tortilla Soup (page 97), Chicken Potpie (page 137), or Chicken Salad (page 77). Another great meal builder is Family-Style Pot Roast (page 141), an easy roast that be turned into calzones another night.

Every recipe is designed to be easy to prepare and can be adapted to suit your family's personal tastes. I added minimal spices in dishes like Slow-Cooker Turkey Chili (page 166) and Family-Style Fajitas (page 154) because I know that kids' palettes can be picky. Some like it hot, and some don't. Feel free to use my recipes as a template, and add your own creativity and personal taste to the dish.

What I have loved most about writing this book was that I have been able to re-create many of the family favorites that I grew up loving when having dinner together wasn't optional. Many of us grew up in an era of valuing the food we eat and taking time to sit down together to share the highlights and lowlights of our day. Today's family looks different, as many of us work, travel, or have multiple after-school activities. I know that dinner every night may not be practical or convenient. But I do hope we start to try to put the emphasis on sharing that time together again, because these are the memories we are creating for our children and this is the foundation we are building for when they raise their own families.

Living with food allergies has been a life-changing experience, but not always in a negative way. It has taught our family to slow down and eat together, because most of the time that is our only choice. Families living with food allergies cannot eat out at restaurants, order in pizza, or use prepackaged convenience foods. I had to learn to cook from scratch when my son was diagnosed with life-threatening food allergies in 2003. I was terrified at this prospect, as I loved to eat but was too "busy" or "distracted" to step foot in the kitchen to make many meals myself. Prior to John's diagnosis I ordered takeout all the time and went out to dinner often. We lived in Chicago, a city packed with amazing restaurants. I never had to cook.

John's diagnosis changed all that, but in a beautiful and wonderful way. I learned that there are few things that I love more than creating and preparing food with love for my family, friends, and neighbors, no matter how busy I am. Sometimes a fast BLT sandwich for supper is all I can get on the table in a hurry, but it's good enough, because even five minutes together for supper is fantastic.

Family meals should always be shared together and be as inclusive as possible. And it really isn't as hard as you might think. It's all about shifting your perspective and making simple and delicious recipes that everyone in your family will love.

I hope you take the recipes from this book and make them your own. Change them and share them any which way you like. This book is for you and your own families, from my little ole kitchen to yours. Happy cooking!

Tips & Tricks

MY SON, JOHN, SUFFERS FROM A FEW BUT NOT ALL OF THESE EIGHT MOST common food allergies: dairy, eggs, peanuts, tree nuts, wheat, soy, shellfish, and fish. The recipes in this book are dairy, egg, nut, legume, and pea free to reflect the allergens we specifically keep out of our kitchen. John's diet is limited as it is, so I try to cook with what I know he can safely eat, which includes other allergens such as soy and wheat. However, many if not most of my recipes are easily adaptable to suit your family's own food allergy concerns.

It is also important to remember that every single time you purchase a product in the grocery store, whether it is something you have used for years or for the first time, you *must* read every ingredient on the label very carefully. Even though it is easier than before to read labels for hidden allergens, it doesn't mean ingredients can't change, and they often do. Food companies may change ingredients or production facilities without any warning. Believe me, it has happened to me more than once. So take the time to check in the store before bringing a potentially life-threatening product into your kitchen.

For this reason, I am not going to give any specific product recommendations because of the risk that any of these products might become unsafe or unsuitable for your family years from now, after this book is printed. I keep an updated list of my favorite brands I currently use on my blog, so if you would like to know what I use in my kitchen, check out www.foodallergymama.com.

MY FAVORITE SUBSTITUTE INGREDIENTS

Soy, rice, sunflower, and coconut milk · We love plain, unsweetened soy milk in our house, but any of these dairy alternatives work well. Use cup for cup in substituting non-dairy milk for dairy.

Dairy-free buttermilk · Buttermilk is the easiest thing to make yourself. Simply mix 1 tablespoon white vinegar or 1 tablespoon fresh lemon juice into 1 cup dairy-free milk. Let the mixture stand for 5 to 10 minutes and proceed with the recipe.

Dairy-free margarine or shortening · Nowadays these two ingredients are easily found at your local grocery store. Check my website for brand recommendations, updated regularly. Use the same measurements, cup for cup, as you would for butter.

Other dairy-free substitutes · Sour cream, cream cheese, and other cheeses are all found in dairy-free versions at Whole Foods and even some local grocery stores. In fact, I can now find all of the above substitutes at many of my neighborhood grocery stores. Read labels carefully, however, especially when it comes to cheeses, because many "soy" cheeses contain milk.

Soy substitutes · We don't have a soy allergy in our house, but many of my readers do. Recipes that contain soy (tofu, soy milk, cream cheese) use coconut milk, coconut oil, or coconut yogurt as a substitute. You also can feel free to try other types of milk, such as rice, oat, hemp, or potato milk. They all work interchangeably with dairy or soy milk.

Egg substitutes · If there's one thing I've learned in all these years of allergy-friendly cooking and baking, it's that eggs are not necessary to many recipes and can easily be swapped out. For every egg in a traditional recipe, I often use 1 tablespoon water, ¼ cup unsweetened applesauce, ¼ cup mashed banana, or ¼ cup tofu, or just leave it out altogether. My preference is to use fruit purees and water in treats or baked recipes and tofu in savory baked egg–type recipes.

Peanut or tree nut substitutes · Sunflower or soy nut butter easily replaces peanut butter in all of my recipes. You could also use almond or cashew butter if you don't have a tree nut allergy.

Wheat flour substitutes · Since my food allergic (FA) son, John, is allergic to many other foods but not to wheat, I safely bake and cook with regular unbleached all-purpose flour. However, most of my recipes can easily be substituted with your favorite all-purpose gluten-free flour blend, cup for cup; add ½ to 1 teaspoon xanthan gum per cup of gluten-free flour blend. Xanthan gum acts as a binder in gluten-free recipes.

MY KITCHEN ESSENTIALS

You really don't need a bunch of special equipment in your kitchen to make fast and easy allergy-friendly meals. But you should consider making your kitchen as completely allergen-free as possible. I never make two separate meals—one that has my son's allergens in it, and one without—for three reasons. First, I don't have the time or energy to do that much cooking. But second, and more important, I don't want to make my son feel excluded in his own home by having us eat separate meals. He faces that enough out in the real world, at friends' houses, birthday parties, and in his school lunchroom. Third, there's also an increased risk of cross-contamination when making one meal with allergen-friendly ingredients and one without. The safest approach is to keep your home as allergy-friendly as possible.

Professional rimmed baking sheets · You'll need two or three of them in various sizes, such as half-sheet (13 x 18 inches) and quarter-sheet (9 x 13). I use my baking sheets for everything from baking cookies to roasting meats and vegetables.

12-inch skillet or stainless steel sauté pan · You will use this for everything from tofu scramble to turkey Sloppy Joes.

2-quart and 4-quart stainless steel saucepans · Perfect for making pizza sauce and soups and for reheating sauces. These are your go-to pots for boiling pasta and gnocchi.

Dutch oven · This is one of my favorite investments I've made in my kitchen. It produces the most delicious soups, stews, and sauces; I've lovingly used mine for many years and it's never failed me. Le Creuset makes the classic Dutch oven, but if you don't want to spend the extra money on this brand, there are less expensive versions on the market.

6-cup blender and 14-cup food processor · Both of these are a must to have in the kitchen for making purees, sauces, smoothies, and pesto.

Immersion blender · Since I started using one of these to puree my soups right in the pot, I have never gone back to pureeing in a blender. It is worth it just for the cleanup alone. Besides, the kids really dig it!

Slotted spoon, wooden spoons, and rubber spatulas · This is all you really need to stir your sauces and pancake batters.

4-cup and 2-cup liquid measuring cups and set of dry measuring cups and measuring spoons · Liquid measuring cups really do serve a purpose, as do the dry, and as I've taught my daughter, you should never mix them up by using liquid for dry and vice versa. If you do, the measurements won't be as accurate. Use the right tools and you'll get the right measurements every time.

Parchment paper · I couldn't survive without this, as I rely on it for perfect cookies, roasted veggies, and popcorn treats. Many readers have asked if they can use wax paper instead of parchment. Wax paper is coated with a layer of wax and doesn't perform well in higher temperatures, while parchment paper is nonstick, produces evenly baked goods, and can be reused.

Waffle iron and pancake griddle · Invest in the best when it comes to these tools because you'll probably use them several times a week. I have various sizes of waffle irons that I love to use; sometimes I like to make little waffles and other times I like to make the larger Belgian kind. For pancakes I use either my cast-iron griddle or nonstick griddle. In a pinch, use a well-seasoned cast-iron skillet.

the recipes

1

❋

Snacks are a part of childhood. As parents we are expected to send in snacks for our kids at school or bring them to sports games and other kid-related activities. Unfortunately, the traditional snacks at the grocery store are usually unsafe for kids with food allergies. And usually they're not even very good.

I wanted to create fun and kid-friendly snacks that everyone loves, not just kids with food allergies. This chapter is filled with everything you need, from after-school snacks to party dips. I promise no one will ever know they're allergy-friendly.

trail mix

I've made this mix with my kids for years. It's the perfect after-school snack, and making it is a fun activity. Put out little bowls of mix-ins—use what I've chosen below or go for whatever you have in the house—and have the kids join in on the fun.

MAKES 8 CUPS

1 cup allergy-friendly mini chocolate chips

4 cups allergy-friendly cereal

1 cup dried cranberries

1 cup raisins

1 cup allergy-friendly mini marshmallows

½ cup sunflower seeds

1 cup allergy-friendly mini pretzels

✳ Set out bowls of each ingredient along with little spoons. Have your children scoop out the ingredients they want into sandwich-size resealable bags, seal, shake, and serve. Or combine everything in one large resealable plastic bag.

party mix

Everyone loves a good snack mix. This is the easiest, most adaptable party mix you'll find. It's also incredibly yummy. Pack it in lunch boxes for a healthy snack or triple the recipe for a great party dish. It stores well in a resealable container for up to a week.

MAKES 3 CUPS

2 tablespoons dairy-free margarine, melted

2½ teaspoons Worcestershire sauce

1 packed teaspoon light brown sugar

¼ teaspoon kosher salt

¼ teaspoon onion powder

¼ teaspoon garlic powder

2 cups allergy-friendly cereal

½ cup allergy-friendly mini pretzels

½ cup dried fruit, such as raisins or cranberries

❋ Preheat the oven to 250°F.

❋ On a rimmed baking sheet, combine the melted margarine, Worcestershire sauce, brown sugar, salt, onion powder, and garlic powder. Stir in the cereal and pretzels and mix well. Spread the mixture in an even layer on the baking sheet and bake 45 to 50 minutes, until toasted. Remove from the oven and cool completely. Add the dried fruit and store in a resealable container for up to a week.

aunt della's soft pretzels

Aunt Della is my husband's adorable and spunky eighty-five-year-old aunt, and I'm very fortunate to call her my aunt too. She's old-school Italian, preferring to make dough for pretzels and calzones by "feeling" her way along rather than using precise measurements. After spending years teaching her own children and grandchildren how to make homemade dough, Aunt Della started teaching a popular after-school enrichment class for elementary children called Dough with Della. It took some prodding from her daughters to get it all written down, but now this favorite recipe of hers has just the right measurements so you can make it at home.

MAKES 16 PRETZELS

> One .25-ounce package active dry yeast
>
> 1½ cups warm water (about 115°F)
>
> 4 to 4¼ cups unbleached all-purpose flour
>
> 1 teaspoon kosher salt
>
> 1 teaspoon sugar
>
> Olive oil
>
> Kosher salt, sea salt, or cinnamon sugar for sprinkling on the pretzels

❋ In a liquid measuring cup, dissolve the yeast in the warm water and let sit for a couple of minutes.

❋ In the bowl of an electric mixer fitted with the dough hook, combine 2 cups of the flour, the salt, and sugar and mix until combined. Add the yeast mixture and beat until smooth. Stir in enough of the remaining flour to form a dough that's pliable and easy to handle.

❋ Turn the dough onto a lightly floured surface and knead for about 5 minutes, until the dough is smooth and easily stretches.

❋ Lightly oil a stainless steel or glass bowl and place the dough in the prepared bowl. Cover with a dish towel and let the dough rise until nearly double in size, about 30 minutes. Punch the dough down and cut it into 16 equal portions.

❋ Preheat the oven to 425°F and line 2 baking sheets with parchment paper.

❋ Roll each portion of dough into a rope about 18 inches long and twist each into a pretzel shape. Place the pretzels on the prepared baking sheets, sprinkle with salt or cinnamon sugar, and bake for about 15 minutes, until the pretzels are golden brown. Remove the pretzels from the baking sheets and cool before serving.

cinnamon-sugar popcorn

This is a great after-school snack, especially when you have kids over for play-dates. Get the little ones to decorate their own brown paper bags and have them fill them with their popcorn snack when it's ready.

SERVES 4

> 3 tablespoons vegetable or canola oil
>
> ½ cup popcorn kernels
>
> ½ teaspoon salt
>
> 2 tablespoons dairy-free margarine
>
> ¼ packed cup light brown sugar
>
> 1½ teaspoons ground cinnamon
>
> ⅛ teaspoon ground nutmeg

❊ Heat the oil in a large heavy saucepan over medium-high heat.

❊ Add the popcorn kernels to the pan, partially cover, and allow the corn to pop, shaking the pan until the popping sounds stop. Remove from the heat, transfer to a large bowl, and sprinkle with the salt.

❊ In a small microwave-safe bowl, combine the margarine, brown sugar, cinnamon, and nutmeg, and heat in the microwave for 30 seconds, or until the margarine is melted. Toss with the popcorn and serve.

rocky road popcorn

This is a fantastic party snack. It's also incredibly easy and fast to make. I like to store it in a large resealable plastic bag in the fridge so it keeps longer.

SERVES 4

3 tablespoons vegetable or canola oil

½ cup popcorn kernels

2 cups allergy-friendly mini marshmallows

One 10-ounce package allergy-friendly mini chocolate chips

✳ Heat the oil in a large heavy saucepan over medium-high heat.

✳ Add the corn kernels to the pan, partially cover, and allow the corn to pop, shaking the pan until the popping sounds stop. Remove from the heat and transfer to a large bowl.

✳ Immediately add the marshmallows and chocolate chips, and stir the mixture with a rubber spatula. The chips should melt from the heat of the popped corn; if they don't, heat the mixture in the microwave for about 20 seconds, until the chips are slightly melted. Let cool, about 10 minutes, stir, and serve.

french onion dip

One of my favorite snacks when I was pregnant with my kids was Ruffles potato chips and French onion dip. These days I try to make healthier options for my kids and serve this dairy-free French onion dip with cut veggies and baked potato chips. It's a great party dip as well as a delicious lunch-box meal.

MAKES 2 CUPS

1 tablespoon extra virgin olive oil

1 tablespoon dairy-free margarine

2 Vidalia onions, finely diced

1 cup dairy-free sour cream

½ cup vegan mayonnaise

¼ teaspoon celery seeds

Kosher salt and pepper

¼ cup finely chopped fresh chives (optional)

❋ In a large skillet, heat the oil and margarine over medium-low heat. Add the onions and sauté for about 20 minutes, stirring occasionally, until the onions are golden brown and caramelized. Transfer the onions to a small bowl and cool completely.

❋ In a medium bowl, combine the sour cream, mayonnaise, celery seeds, caramelized onions, and salt and pepper to taste. Add the chopped chives, if using.

❋ Cover and refrigerate for at least 1 hour to allow the flavors to blend together. Serve the dip with baked potato chips or fresh cut veggies. The dip can be stored for up to 2 days in the refrigerator.

dill dip

My sister, Chris, created this delicious dip. My kids went crazy for it when she served it as an appetizer for Thanksgiving. It's also perfect to pack in lunches with fresh veggies or as an after-school snack.

MAKES 1 CUP

1 cup dairy-free sour cream

1 tablespoon dried dill weed

1 teaspoon minced garlic, or ½ teaspoon garlic powder

1 teaspoon minced onion, or ½ teaspoon dried onion powder

½ teaspoon kosher salt

¼ teaspoon freshly ground pepper

Assorted fresh cut vegetables for serving

✳ Combine all the ingredients in the bowl of an electric mixer fitted with the paddle attachment or a food processor. Mix very well, transfer to a container, and refrigerate for at least 1 hour before serving.

chipotle mayonnaise

My husband loves this dip and puts it on practically everything. I love it with baked sweet potato wedges, and my husband's favorite way of eating it is on a hamburger or BLT. It is also a fantastic dip for fresh cut vegetables or with baked pita chips. Use just one chipotle if you or your kids like less heat. You'll find canned chipotle chiles in adobo sauce in the Mexican food aisle at your grocery store.

MAKES 1½ CUPS

1 cup vegan mayonnaise

¼ cup dairy-free sour cream

2 canned chipotles in adobo sauce

1 tablespoon adobo sauce from the chipotle chile can
(omit if you want less heat)

1 tablespoon freshly squeezed lime juice

Kosher salt and freshly ground pepper

❋ Combine the mayonnaise, sour cream, chipotles, adobo sauce, lime juice, and salt and pepper to taste in a blender or food processor and blend until creamy. Store covered in the refrigerator up to 1 week.

crostini with pesto

Crostini is one of the easiest appetizers to make and can be topped with anything your family likes. Nut- and dairy-free pesto is a great condiment for sandwiches and breads as well as pasta. It also freezes well and is fantastic as a garnish on vegetable soup. The pesto itself can be kept in the freezer in small freezer bags for up to two months.

SERVES 4 TO 6

CROSTINI

1 allergy-friendly or gluten-free baguette

2 tablespoons extra virgin olive oil

Kosher salt and freshly ground pepper

PESTO

2 packed cups fresh basil leaves

½ cup extra virgin olive oil

2 medium garlic cloves, chopped

½ teaspoon kosher salt

¼ teaspoon freshly ground pepper

2 tablespoons dairy-free margarine, softened

⅓ cup grated dairy-free Parmesan cheese

❋ Preheat the oven to 375°F and line a large rimmed baking sheet with parchment paper.

❋ Cut the bread into ¼-inch slices and place the slices on the prepared baking sheet. Brush the tops with the oil and season with salt and pepper. Place in the oven and bake for 10 to 15 minutes, until toasted.

✳ **WHILE THE BREAD IS IN THE OVEN, MAKE THE PESTO:** In a food processor or blender, combine the basil, oil, garlic, salt, and pepper and process until blended. Pour the mixture into a bowl and stir in the softened margarine and cheese. Spread on the crostini and serve.

tomato bruschetta

This is the perfect appetizer to serve in the summertime when fresh tomatoes and basil are in abundance at the farmers' market.

SERVES 4

8 slices allergy-friendly or gluten-free country bread or baguette

2 garlic cloves, cut in half

2 tablespoons extra virgin olive oil

2 large tomatoes, seeded and diced

Kosher salt and freshly ground pepper

6 to 8 fresh basil leaves, torn

✳ In a grill pan or on a gas grill, lightly grill the bread slices until grill marks appear, about 5 minutes. Rub the garlic halves on the bread slices and drizzle with the oil.

✳ Place the tomatoes in a medium bowl and season with salt and pepper to taste. Top each grilled bread slice with about ¼ cup of tomato mixture, sprinkle the basil on top, and serve warm or at room temperature.

garlic bread

Garlic bread is a must when serving pasta at our house. My kids love it and fight over the last piece every time.

SERVES 4

1 allergy-friendly or gluten-free baguette, sliced in half lengthwise
5 tablespoons dairy-free margarine
4 large garlic cloves, finely minced

✳ Preheat the oven to 450°F and position a rack in the top of the oven. Line a rimmed baking sheet with foil.

✳ Heat the margarine in a microwave-safe bowl for 30 seconds, or until melted. Add the garlic to the margarine and spread the mixture evenly over the cut sides of the bread. Put the halves back together and place on the prepared baking sheet.

✳ Place the bread in the oven and bake for 10 minutes, or until it is starting to toast. Open the halves so that the buttered side faces up, heat up the broiler, and broil for about 2 minutes, watching the broiler carefully, as the bread can burn very quickly. Remove from the oven when the bread is lightly toasted and golden. Cut into slices and serve.

baked potato skins

Baked potato skins are a delicious party snack that everyone loves, and this recipe is much healthier than other versions. Feel free to adjust the toppings to whatever you and your family like.

SERVES 6

6 small baking potatoes, scrubbed
¾ cup shredded dairy-free cheddar cheese
4 slices bacon, cooked and crumbled
½ cup dairy-free sour cream
2 tablespoons chopped fresh chives (optional)
Kosher salt and freshly ground pepper

❊ Preheat the oven to 425°F.

❊ Pierce the potatoes all over with a fork, place in the oven, and bake for 45 to 50 minutes, until done. Remove from the oven when softened enough to be pierced, then pierce with a fork and cool until the potatoes can be handled without burning your hands.

❊ Turn on the broiler.

❊ Cut the potatoes in half lengthwise and scoop out the potato flesh, leaving a ⅛-inch shell. (Reserve the potato flesh for another use.) Place the potatoes on a rimmed baking sheet, skin sides down. Divide the cheese and bacon evenly among the insides of the shells.

❊ Place the filled potato shells under the broiler and broil for 2 to 3 minutes, until the cheese is melted and the potato skins are crisped. Top the skins with the sour cream and chives, if using. Season with salt and pepper to taste and serve immediately.

kale chips

I love kale, but getting my kids to love it as much as I do has been challenging. They would love it in my vegetable soup but rarely on its own. That is, until they tried these kale chips. Kale chips are a popular snack right now, and every book seems to have a tried-and-true recipe. There's no rocket science here, just delicious kale, salt, and a little paprika for added color and taste.

SERVES 4

2 bunches Tuscan kale
1½ teaspoons extra virgin olive oil
½ teaspoon paprika
Kosher or sea salt

❋ Preheat the oven to 300°F and line 2 baking sheets with parchment paper.

❋ Tear 2-inch pieces of kale away from the stems and place on the prepared baking sheets. Drizzle evenly with the oil and sprinkle with the paprika and salt to taste. Toss the kale with your hands to evenly coat.

❋ Place in the oven and bake for 15 to 20 minutes, until the leaves are crisp.

oma's warm milk

Oma was one of those women you meet just once in a lifetime. She was my best friend Stacey's grandmother, and I had the great honor of getting to know her one summer when Stacey came to Chicago to live with her for a few months. Oma's cure for anything from a sore throat to a broken heart was warm, soothing milk. Sadly, she passed away recently at age ninety-four. Her recipe was simple yet timeless, and her family and mine still make little cups of warmed milk to soothe our souls.

SERVES 2

2 cups non-dairy milk
2 tablespoons honey
2 cinnamon sticks (optional)

✳ Place the non-dairy milk in a small saucepan over low heat. When just barely warmed through, ladle into 2 mugs and stir 1 tablespoon honey into each mug. Serve with a cinnamon stick, if using.

cinnamon toast

There is probably no other recipe in this entire book that speaks more to my heart than cinnamon toast. It was the one thing that made me feel better when I was sick as a kid (and still does as a grownup). It was the one thing I ate every morning and night when living on a kibbutz in Israel. And it is still the one thing I often eat now along with my hot tea at night. I'm not a food snob and I am not going to tell you there's only one way to make great cinnamon toast. Feel free to simply toast your bread in the toaster or make your own cinnamon sugar mixture. There's no wrong way—this is just my way.

SERVES 2

½ cup sugar

1 teaspoon ground cinnamon

4 slices allergy-friendly or gluten-free white bread

4 tablespoons dairy-free margarine, softened

❋ Preheat the broiler.

❋ In a small bowl, combine the sugar and cinnamon.

❋ Place the bread on a baking sheet and lightly toast under the broiler, watching closely so as not to burn the bread.

❋ Remove the bread from the oven and spread 1 tablespoon margarine over each piece of bread. Sprinkle the cinnamon-sugar mixture evenly over the bread and return the slices to the broiler. Toast for about another minute, until the bread is just starting to bubble and glisten. Remove from the oven, cut the slices in half, and serve.

2

❊

I've always been a breakfast kind of girl, and it has always been my favorite meal. My kids feel the same way, and they always seem to want breakfast-type foods for lunch and dinner too!

Making a warm and delicious breakfast is so much more special than pouring a box of cereal into a bowl. Who doesn't love cinnamon-scented pancakes or a fruity and frosty smoothie? And for food-allergic kids, making yummy chocolate donuts at home is the only way to go (and they're so much better than donut shops, I promise). These breakfast treats will certainly make breakfast at home easy and memorable.

tropical smoothie

This is the perfect smoothie to serve your kids during the cold and flu season, as it is packed with vitamin C and antioxidants. I like to put in a few drops of liquid vitamins, particularly vitamin D, for an extra boost.

SERVES 4

1 cup orange juice

½ cup soy or rice milk

¼ cup dairy-free plain yogurt

½ cup fresh or frozen strawberries

½ cup fresh or frozen pineapple cubes

½ cup fresh or frozen mango cubes

❋ Place all the ingredients in a blender and blend until smooth. If using fresh fruit, throw a few ice cubes into the blender too. Serve immediately in glasses.

powerhouse smoothie

My preteen daughter, Chloe, claims she's too busy to eat breakfast, so I made this yummy smoothie just for her. It combines the powerful health benefits of pomegranate, berries, and soy or rice milk. Drops of liquid vitamins are a great addition too.

SERVES 4

1¼ cups pomegranate juice

1¼ cups soy or rice milk

1 cup fresh or frozen strawberries

1 cup fresh or frozen blueberries

❋ Place all the ingredients in a blender and blend until smooth. If using fresh berries, throw a few ice cubes into the blender too. Serve immediately in glasses.

healthier granola

The granolas you find in most grocery stores often contain nuts and are packed with oil and sugar. We've never bought them, and I never thought I could make a yummy granola until I made this one. It is easily adaptable to whatever you and your family like.

SERVES 4

½ cup soy butter, sunflower butter, or other nut butter alternative

½ cup honey

2 tablespoons vegetable or canola oil

1 teaspoon vanilla extract

1 teaspoon ground cinnamon

3 cups old-fashioned rolled oats

1 teaspoon kosher salt

2 cups dried fruit, such as raisins, currants, golden raisins, blueberries, cranberries, or banana chips

✳ Preheat the oven to 300°F and line a baking sheet with parchment paper.

✳ In a medium saucepan, combine the soy butter, honey, oil, vanilla, and cinnamon. Place over low heat and stir until the mixture is smooth.

✳ In a medium bowl, combine the oats and salt. Add the wet mixture to the oats and stir well; use your hands if needed.

✳ Spread the granola mixture onto the prepared pan and bake for 15 to 20 minutes, until the granola is lightly browned and toasted. Remove from the oven, cool on the sheet, and add the dried fruit. The granola keeps for up to 1 week in an airtight container.

easy scottish-style porridge

This is an oatmeal lover's special treat, and a wonderful breakfast or brunch dish to serve your family or guests. It's written that the tradition in Scotland is to never serve hot porridge with hot milk. In this version, cold soy or rice milk is swirled into the finished oats, and then they're sweetened with a little honey, brown sugar, and sweet spices.

SERVES 4

4 cups water

¾ teaspoon salt

2 cups quick-cooking (not instant) oats

⅓ cup cold soy or rice milk

¼ packed cup light brown sugar

2½ tablespoons honey

½ teaspoon ground cinnamon

¼ teaspoon ground nutmeg

1 cup raisins or other dried fruit (optional)

✳ In a large saucepan, combine the water and salt and bring to a boil over medium-high heat. Add the oats and cook for about 1½ minutes, stirring constantly. Remove from the heat and swirl in the soy milk, brown sugar, honey, cinnamon, nutmeg, and raisins, if using.

vegetable strata

Everyone loves a great make-ahead, morning-of breakfast casserole. Even though this strata is egg-free, no one would ever guess it. It's delicious, colorful, and very easy to make. It takes only about ten minutes to prepare, so I typically will just make and bake it when I need it. However, if you want to make it the night before, store the blended tofu custard separately and pour it over the bread and vegetable mixture just before you're about to bake it.

SERVES 6

1 large loaf allergy-friendly or gluten-free French bread, cut into ¾-inch pieces

2 tablespoons extra virgin olive oil

1 tablespoon dairy-free margarine

½ cup diced onion

2 cups diced red, yellow, orange, or green peppers (preferably a combination)

2 cups sliced mushrooms

1 teaspoon kosher salt

½ teaspoon freshly ground pepper

2 packed cups baby spinach

1 cup shredded dairy-free mozzarella cheese

One 14-ounce package silken tofu (about 1½ cups), drained

1 cup soy or rice milk

1 teaspoon Dijon-style mustard

¼ teaspoon dry mustard

¾ teaspoon ground turmeric

½ teaspoon Worcestershire sauce (omit for soy allergies)

✳ Preheat the oven to 375°F and spray a 9 x 13-inch baking dish with dairy-free cooking spray. Place the bread cubes in the prepared baking dish and set aside.

✳ Heat the oil and margarine in a large skillet over medium-high heat. Add the onion, peppers, mushrooms, salt, and pepper, and sauté for 5 to 8 minutes, until softened. Stir in the spinach and cook until wilted. Remove from the heat and pour the mixture over the bread cubes. Sprinkle the shredded cheese on top.

✳ In a blender or food processor, combine the tofu, soy milk, mustards, turmeric, and Worcestershire sauce and process until combined. Pour the tofu mixture over the bread and vegetable mixture. Lightly stir just until the tofu custard is combined with the bread cubes.

✳ Bake for 35 to 45 minutes, until the top is beginning to brown. Remove from the oven and let stand for a few minutes before cutting into pieces and serving.

tofu and veggie scramble

My kids love this dish with toast. It's super-healthy and can be made with any variation of veggies you have on hand in the fridge. Feel free to add a little more cayenne if your family likes your scramble spicy. It also doubles as the perfect "breakfast for dinner" entrée.

SERVES 4

1 tablespoon vegetable or canola oil

¼ cup finely diced onion

½ cup finely diced green pepper

½ cup finely diced red pepper

½ cup diced mushrooms

1 medium tomato, seeded and diced

¼ to ½ teaspoon cayenne pepper

¼ to ½ teaspoon ground cumin

¾ teaspoon kosher salt

¼ teaspoon freshly ground pepper

One 14-ounce package extra-firm tofu, drained and broken into pieces

✳ Heat the oil in a 10-inch skillet over medium heat. Add the onion, green pepper, red pepper, mushrooms, tomato, cayenne, cumin, salt, and pepper and sauté for 5 to 7 minutes, until the vegetables are slightly softened. Add the tofu pieces and cook for an additional 3 to 4 minutes, stirring a couple of times, until the tofu is warmed through. Serve over toast.

VARIATION: Breakfast Burrito

✳ Fill warmed allergy-friendly or gluten-free tortillas with the tofu scramble mixture and top with your favorite salsa, dairy-free cheddar cheese, and dairy-free sour cream. Fold up the sides, roll it up, tuck the seams under, and serve.

classic french toast

I can't think about French toast without thinking of my mom. In my early college years I worked as a leasing agent full time and went to college at night and on my days off. So the only time I got to hang out with my sisters and mom was on Tuesdays at our favorite diner in Chicago, Mitchell's. I learned a lot from that diner about what makes a great French toast: start with great bread, and infuse the dipping liquid with as much sweetness as possible. This egg, dairy, and nut free version reminds me of those fantastic French toast Tuesdays. Homemade bread that is slightly dry is best, but you can use any of your favorite allergy-friendly breads; I like to use Italian Vienna bread.

SERVES 6

2 cups soy or rice milk

¼ cup unbleached all-purpose flour or gluten-free flour blend

2 packed tablespoons light brown sugar

1 teaspoon ground cinnamon

1 teaspoon vanilla extract

1 tablespoon honey

6 thick slices allergy-friendly or gluten-free bread

Maple syrup and confectioners' sugar

✻ Preheat an electric griddle to 400°F or heat a cast-iron skillet over medium-high heat. Spray the surface of the griddle with dairy-free cooking spray.

✻ While the griddle is heating up, whisk together the soy milk, flour, brown sugar, cinnamon, vanilla, and honey. Pour the mixture into a shallow bowl and

dip both sides of each bread slice in the mixture, coating well. Remove the bread slices from the soy milk mixture, allowing the excess to drip.

❊ Place the bread slices on the hot griddle and cook for 3 to 4 minutes on each side, until browned. Serve topped with maple syrup and confectioners' sugar.

cinnamon spice pancakes

These are a healthy and hearty alternative to your standard buttermilk pancake recipe. I love fluffy pancakes, but if you like yours thinner and flatter, simply add a few more tablespoons of soy or rice milk.

SERVES 4

1 cup unbleached all-purpose flour or gluten-free flour blend

1 cup whole-wheat flour (alternatively use only all-purpose flour or a gluten-free flour blend)

1 cup old-fashioned rolled oats (or use gluten-free oats)

¼ packed cup light brown sugar

1¼ tablespoons baking powder

1 teaspoon ground cinnamon

½ teaspoon salt

¼ teaspoon ground nutmeg

⅛ teaspoon ground cloves

2 cups soy or rice milk

¼ cup vegetable or canola oil

2 tablespoons water

1 teaspoon vanilla extract

❋ Heat an electric griddle to 400°F or a cast-iron skillet over medium-high heat. Coat the surface of the griddle with dairy-free cooking spray.

❋ In a medium bowl, combine the flours, oats, brown sugar, baking powder, cinnamon, salt, nutmeg, and cloves using a wire whisk. In a liquid measuring cup, whisk together the soy milk, oil, water, and vanilla. Pour the liquid mixture into the dry mixture and stir until just combined. Do not overmix; some lumps are fine.

❋ Use a ¼-cup measuring cup to pour pancake batter onto the hot griddle. After a minute or 2, or when bubbles start to form on the surface, flip the pancakes over and cook for another minute. Repeat with the remaining batter. You can keep the pancakes warm in a 200°F oven as you go along.

FREEZER TIP • Place leftover pancakes in a plastic freezer bag and freeze for up to a month. Reheat in a 200°F oven or in the microwave or toaster.

lemon blueberry pancakes

The best pancakes I ever had were at a bed and breakfast inn in South Haven, Michigan, the "unofficial" blueberry capital of the world. This pancake is inspired by that amazing breakfast. It is bursting with fresh blueberries in every bite. If you love blueberries, this will become your favorite pancake.

SERVES 4

1 cup soy or rice buttermilk (see page 6)

¼ cup vegetable or canola oil

2 tablespoons water

1¼ teaspoons vanilla extract

1 tablespoon freshly grated lemon zest

1 tablespoon freshly squeezed lemon juice

1½ cups unbleached all-purpose flour or gluten-free flour

2 tablespoons sugar

1 tablespoon baking powder

½ teaspoon salt

¾ cup to 1 cup fresh blueberries

❋ Heat an electric griddle to 400°F or a cast-iron skillet over medium-high heat. Coat the surface of the griddle with dairy-free cooking spray.

❋ In a large liquid measuring cup, whisk together the soy buttermilk, oil, water, vanilla, lemon zest, and lemon juice. In a medium bowl, combine the flour, sugar, baking powder, and salt using a wire whisk. Add the buttermilk mixture to the flour mixture and stir until just combined; a few lumps are fine. Add the blueberries (more or less, depending on how many blueberries you like in your pancakes).

❈ Use a ¼-cup measuring cup to pour pancake batter onto the hot griddle. After a minute or 2, when bubbles start to form on the surface, flip the pancakes over and cook for another minute. Repeat with the remaining batter. You can keep the pancakes warm in a 200°F oven as you go along.

FREEZER TIP • Place leftover pancakes in a plastic freezer bag and freeze for up to a month. Reheat in a 200°F oven, the microwave, or a toaster.

gingerbread waffles

There are few things that smell more heavenly than gingerbread baking. These waffles are no exception. I love to cut them up into sticks and serve with real maple syrup for dipping. I also love to double this recipe, as it freezes well and makes a deliciously warm breakfast on a chilly morning.

MAKES 8 LARGE OR 16 SMALL WAFFLES

2¼ cups unbleached all-purpose flour
or gluten-free flour blend

2 packed tablespoons light brown sugar

1⅛ tablespoons baking powder

2⅛ teaspoons ground ginger

1 teaspoon ground cinnamon

⅛ teaspoon ground nutmeg

⅛ teaspoon ground cloves

½ teaspoon salt

1¼ cups soy or rice milk

6 tablespoons vegetable or canola oil

¼ cup molasses

1 teaspoon vanilla extract

2 tablespoons water

Warmed maple syrup for serving

❋ Preheat a waffle iron according to the manufacturer's instructions while you prepare the batter.

❋ In a medium bowl, combine the flour, brown sugar, baking powder, ginger, cinnamon, nutmeg, cloves, and salt, using a wire whisk.

✳ In a liquid measuring cup, combine the soy milk, oil, molasses, vanilla, and water. Add to the dry ingredients and stir just until combined. Let stand for about 5 minutes.

✳ Coat the waffle iron with dairy-free cooking spray and pour some batter into the heated waffle iron (the amount will vary depending on the size of your waffle iron) and cook according to the manufacturer's instructions. Repeat with the remaining batter until it's used up. Keep warm in a 200°F oven if you like. Cut into sticks and serve with warm maple syrup.

FREEZER TIP • Freeze in resealable plastic bags for up to 2 months. Reheat in the toaster or a 200°F oven for 10 minutes.

double chocolate waffles

These little chocolate wonder waffles are perfect for special mornings like Valentine's Day and birthday breakfast-in-bed celebrations, or even just to coax your kids out of bed on a Monday morning.

MAKES 20 WAFFLES

> **2 cups unbleached all-purpose flour or gluten-free flour blend**
> **½ cup unsweetened cocoa powder**
> **½ cup sugar**
> **4 teaspoons baking powder**
> **¾ teaspoon salt**
> **1¾ cups soy or rice milk**
> **¼ cup vegetable or canola oil**
> **¼ cup water**
> **2 teaspoons vanilla extract**
> **½ cup allergy-friendly chocolate chips**
> **Sliced fresh strawberries (optional)**
> **Confectioners' sugar for dusting**

✳ Preheat a waffle iron according to the manufacturer's instructions while you prepare the batter.

✳ In a medium bowl, combine the flour, cocoa powder, sugar, baking powder, and salt using a wire whisk. In a large liquid measuring cup, whisk together the soy milk, oil, water, and vanilla. Add the soy milk mixture to the flour mixture and stir just until combined. Use a rubber spatula to stir in the chocolate chips.

✳ Coat the waffle iron with dairy-free cooking spray, and depending on the size of your waffle iron, pour about ⅓ cup batter onto the waffle iron and

cook according to the manufacturer's instructions. Repeat with the remaining batter until it's used up. Keep warm in a 200°F oven if you like. Serve with fresh berries, if using, and a dusting of confectioners' sugar.

FREEZER TIP • Freeze in resealable plastic bags for up to 2 months. Reheat in the toaster or a 200°F oven for 10 minutes.

banana chocolate chip waffles

These waffles are reminiscent of the delicious banana chocolate chip muffins in my first book. They're one of my kids' favorite waffles.

MAKES 20 WAFFLES

1²/₃ cups soy or rice milk

6 tablespoons vegetable or canola oil

2 tablespoons water

1 cup mashed ripe bananas (about 2 bananas)

2 cups unbleached all-purpose flour or gluten-free flour blend

2 tablespoons granulated sugar
or 2 packed tablespoons light brown sugar

1 tablespoon baking powder

¼ teaspoon salt

½ cup allergy-friendly chocolate chips

❋ Preheat a waffle iron according to the manufacturer's instructions while you prepare the batter.

❋ In a large liquid measuring cup, combine the soy milk, oil, water, and banana using a wire whisk. In a medium bowl, combine the flour, sugar, baking powder, and salt using a wire whisk. Add the liquid ingredients to the dry; stir until just combined. Stir in the chocolate chips with a rubber spatula.

❋ Coat the waffle iron with dairy-free cooking spray, and depending upon the size of the iron, ladle about ⅓ cup batter on the hot iron and cook according to the manufacturer's instructions. Repeat with the remaining batter until it's used up. Keep warm in a 200ºF oven if you like.

FREEZER TIP • Freeze in resealable plastic bags for up to 2 months. Reheat in the toaster or a 200ºF oven for 10 minutes.

morning glory muffins

One of my favorite bakeries, Tag's in Evanston, Illinois, serves the best morning glory muffins. They traditionally contain nuts, but this version is completely dairy, egg, and nut free.

MAKES 12 MUFFINS

½ cup vegetable or canola oil

½ cup soy or rice milk

2 tablespoons water

2½ teaspoons vanilla extract

2 cups unbleached all-purpose flour or gluten-free flour blend

¾ packed cup light brown sugar

2 teaspoons baking soda

2 teaspoons ground cinnamon

¼ teaspoon ground nutmeg

¼ teaspoon salt

1 cup shredded peeled carrots

¾ cup shredded peeled apples (I use Granny Smith, but any variety will do)

½ cup raisins

❋ Preheat the oven to 350°F and coat a 12-cup muffin pan with dairy-free cooking spray.

❋ In a small bowl, combine the oil, soy milk, water, and vanilla with a wire whisk. In a medium bowl, combine the flour, brown sugar, baking soda, cinnamon, nutmeg, and salt using a wire whisk. Add the soy milk mixture to the flour mixture and stir with a rubber spatula until just combined. Stir in the carrots and apples until completely mixed in, then stir in the raisins.

❋ Use a cookie scooper to divide the muffin batter evenly among the prepared muffin cups. Bake for 18 to 22 minutes, until lightly browned and a toothpick inserted in the center comes out clean. Cool completely in the pan and store up to three days in an airtight container.

double chocolate chip muffins

These are the ultimate muffins to serve in the morning, or even as a special after-school snack. What kid wouldn't love a little bit of chocolate in the morning?

MAKES 12 MUFFINS

1½ cups soy or rice milk

⅓ cup vegetable or canola oil

2 tablespoons water

1¼ teaspoons vanilla extract

2 cups unbleached all-purpose flour or gluten-free flour blend

⅔ cup unsweetened cocoa powder

½ cup sugar

2 teaspoons baking soda

¼ teaspoon salt

½ cup allergy-friendly chocolate chips

TOPPING (OPTIONAL)

¼ cup allergy-friendly chocolate chips

❋ Preheat the oven to 400°F and coat a 12-cup muffin pan generously with dairy-free cooking spray.

❋ In a medium bowl, whisk together the soy milk, oil, water, and vanilla. In a large bowl, combine the flour, cocoa powder, sugar, baking soda, and salt using a wire whisk. Add the soy milk mixture to the flour mixture and stir with a rubber spatula until just combined. Stir in the chocolate chips.

❋ Divide the muffin batter evenly among the prepared muffin cups. Sprinkle with the topping, if using. Bake for 15 to 18 minutes, until a cake tester or inserted toothpick comes out clean. Cool in the pan for 5 minutes and serve.

pumpkin chocolate chip muffins

This is a delicious muffin to make in the fall or during the holidays. The recipe makes a slightly larger batch than the standard 12-cup muffin pan, which is great, as that means there's more to pass around! Use one 12-cup muffin pan and half of a second one.

MAKES 18

1 cup dairy-free margarine

1½ cups sugar, plus more for sprinkling

¼ cup water

1 teaspoon vanilla extract

One 15-ounce can pumpkin puree
(not pie filling)

3 cups unbleached all-purpose flour or
gluten-free flour blend

2 teaspoons baking soda

1 teaspoon salt

1¼ teaspoons ground cinnamon

1 teaspoon ground nutmeg

¼ teaspoon ground cloves

¼ teaspoon ground ginger

1½ cups allergy-friendly chocolate chips

❋ Preheat the oven to 350°F and coat 18 muffin cups with dairy-free cooking spray.

❋ In the bowl of an electric mixer fitted with the paddle attachment, combine the margarine, sugar, water, vanilla, and pumpkin puree and mix thoroughly.

❋ In a medium bowl, combine the flour, baking soda, salt, cinnamon, nutmeg, cloves, and ginger, using a wire whisk. Add to the margarine mixture

and mix on low speed until combined. Stir in the chocolate chips, using a rubber spatula.

❋ Use a cookie scooper to divide the batter evenly among the muffin cups. Sprinkle the tops with sugar and bake for 18 to 25 minutes, until a cake tester or inserted toothpick comes out clean. Cool slightly in the pan and serve.

chocolate banana bread

This bread is delicious smeared with a little soy or sunflower butter.

SERVES 8

½ cup dairy-free margarine, melted

1¾ cups mashed ripe bananas (about 3 large bananas)

2 tablespoons water

1½ teaspoons vanilla extract

1¾ cups unbleached all-purpose flour or gluten-free flour blend

¼ cup unsweetened cocoa powder

¾ cup sugar

1 teaspoon baking powder

½ teaspoon baking soda

¼ teaspoon salt

¾ cup allergy-friendly chocolate chips

❀ Preheat the oven to 350°F and coat a 9-inch loaf pan generously with dairy-free cooking spray.

❀ In a small bowl, combine the melted margarine, bananas, water, and vanilla using a wooden spoon. In a medium bowl, combine the flour, cocoa powder, sugar, baking powder, baking soda, and salt using a wire whisk. Add the margarine mixture to the flour mixture and stir with a rubber spatula until just combined. Stir in the chocolate chips.

❀ Pour the batter into the prepared loaf pan and bake for 50 to 60 minutes, until a inserted toothpick in the middle comes out clean. Cool in the pan and serve.

spiced apple bundt cake

This is the perfect cake to serve in the fall when apples are plentiful. It smells delicious baking away in the oven.

SERVES 6

1¼ cups granulated sugar

¾ cup vegetable or canola oil

¾ cup unsweetened applesauce

1 tablespoon vanilla extract

3 cups unbleached all-purpose flour or gluten-free flour blend

1 tablespoon baking soda

1 tablespoon ground cinnamon

1 teaspoon salt

⅛ teaspoon ground nutmeg

3 cups peeled, grated apples (about 4, any variety; I love Granny Smith and Braeburn)

Zest and juice of ½ lemon

Confectioners' sugar for sprinkling

❋ Preheat the oven to 350°F and coat a Bundt pan with dairy-free cooking spray.

❋ In the bowl of an electric mixer fitted with the paddle attachment, combine the granulated sugar, oil, applesauce, and vanilla and mix until combined.

❋ In a medium bowl, combine the flour, baking soda, cinnamon, salt, and nutmeg using a wire whisk. Add to the sugar and oil mixture and mix thoroughly, about 2 minutes.

❋ In a separate medium bowl, combine the apples with the lemon zest and juice. Use a rubber spatula to fold the apples into the sugar-flour mixture. Pour the batter into the prepared pan and bake for about 1 hour, until the top is golden brown and a cake tester or toothpick inserted in the middle comes out clean.

❋ Cool for 10 minutes in the pan on a wire rack, then loosen the cake from the pan and turn it out onto a serving platter. Sprinkle with confectioners' sugar.

easiest coffee cake

This is the easiest coffee cake to make with your kids. I promise it will be gone the day it is made.

SERVES 6

2½ cups unbleached all-purpose flour or gluten-free flour blend

1¾ packed cups light brown sugar

¼ teaspoon salt

⅔ cup dairy-free shortening

2 teaspoons baking powder

½ teaspoon baking soda

1 teaspoon ground cinnamon

½ teaspoon ground nutmeg

1 cup dairy-free buttermilk (see page 6)

2 tablespoons water

1 teaspoon vanilla extract

✳ Preheat the oven to 375°F and coat a 9 x 13-inch Pyrex dish with dairy-free cooking spray.

✳ In the bowl of an electric mixer fitted with the paddle attachment, combine the flour, brown sugar, and salt. Cut in the shortening with your fingers or a pastry blender until it resembles coarse crumbs. Reserve ½ cup of the mixture to be used as the crumb topping later.

✳ Add the baking powder, baking soda, cinnamon, and nutmeg to the remaining crumbs in the mixing bowl and stir until combined.

✳ Whisk together the buttermilk, water, and vanilla in a small bowl and add to the dry mixture. Do not overmix; a few lumps are fine.

✳ Pour the batter into the prepared baking dish and sprinkle with the reserved ½ cup crumb topping. Bake for 30 to 35 minutes, until a cake tester or toothpick comes out clean and the cake is lightly browned. Cool in the pan 5 to 10 minutes and serve warm.

blueberry coffee cake

I love how the blueberry flavor bursts through the crumb cake. This is a great all-day snack cake.

SERVES 6

¼ cup dairy-free margarine, softened

½ cup sugar

1 tablespoon water

1 teaspoon lemon zest

1 teaspoon freshly squeezed lemon juice

1½ cups unbleached all-purpose flour or gluten-free flour blend

1½ teaspoons baking powder

½ teaspoon baking soda

¼ teaspoon salt

½ cup dairy-free buttermilk (see page 6)

2 cups fresh or frozen blueberries

CRUMB TOPPING

1¼ cups unbleached all-purpose flour or gluten-free flour blend

¾ packed cup light brown sugar

½ cup cold dairy-free margarine, cut into chunks

❋ Preheat the oven to 350°F and generously coat a 9-inch square Pyrex baking dish with dairy-free cooking spray.

❋ In the bowl of an electric mixer fitted with the paddle attachment, combine the margarine and sugar and mix until fluffy. Add the water, lemon zest, and lemon juice. In a separate bowl, combine the flour, baking powder, baking soda, and salt using a wire whisk. Alternate adding the flour mixture and the buttermilk to the margarine mixture, combining thoroughly before each addition. Gently fold in the blueberries, using a rubber spatula. Spread the batter into the prepared baking dish.

❋ **TO MAKE THE CRUMB TOPPING,** combine the flour and brown sugar using a wire whisk. Cut in the cold margarine with your fingers until crumbly and there are still large chunks of margarine in the mixture. Sprinkle the crumb mixture evenly over the batter and bake for 45 to 55 minutes, until a cake tester comes out clean and the crumb topping is lightly browned. Place on a wire rack and cool completely before serving.

vanilla mini long johns

I get together with my childhood friends every couple of months; I love them dearly. Since we were young, I've shared my obsession of buying gas station treats like Honey Buns and long johns with them. It was always a blast and a great memory, and I really wanted my food-allergic son, John, to know what the hype was all about. That's why I came up with this recipe. These are best eaten the day they're made.

MAKES 20

3½ cups unbleached all-purpose flour or gluten-free flour blend

¼ cup sugar

¾ teaspoon salt

One .25-ounce package active dry yeast

¼ cup warm water (about 115°F)

1 cup soy or rice milk

¼ cup dairy-free margarine

1 tablespoon water

1 teaspoon vanilla extract

Vegetable or canola oil for frying

VANILLA GLAZE

3 cups confectioners' sugar

5 to 6 tablespoons soy or rice milk

1 tablespoon vanilla extract

❋ In the bowl of an electric mixer fitted with the dough hook, combine 2 cups of the flour, the sugar, and salt.

❋ In a measuring cup, dissolve the yeast in the ¼ cup warm water and mix with a whisk.

✳ In a small saucepan, heat the soy milk, margarine, 1 tablespoon water, and vanilla over low heat until the mixture is just warm, about 115°F.

✳ Add the warmed milk mixture and the yeast mixture to the flour mixture and beat on medium speed until the flour is incorporated into the wet ingredients, scraping down the sides as needed. Add the remaining 1½ cups flour and mix for another 1 to 2 minutes, or until the dough is smooth and pliable.

✳ Coat a medium bowl with dairy-free cooking spray and turn the dough into the bowl. Cover with plastic wrap and let rise until doubled in bulk, about 1 hour. Punch down and turn onto a lightly floured surface. Roll the dough into an 8 x 12-inch rectangle and use a bench scraper or knife to cut 4 x 1-inch rectangles. Place these about an inch apart from one another on a baking sheet lined with parchment paper, cover, and let rise for an additional 20 minutes.

✳ **MEANWHILE, MAKE THE VANILLA GLAZE:** Combine the confectioners' sugar, 5 tablespoons of the soy milk, and the vanilla in a medium bowl. Stir with a small whisk or spoon until the glaze is creamy, adding the remaining tablespoon soy milk if needed.

✳ To fry the long johns, pour enough oil into a Dutch oven or heavy-bottomed pot to go 3 inches up the sides. Heat to 380°F, as measured on a candy thermometer. Fry the risen long johns in the hot oil, 3 or 4 at a time, making sure not to overcrowd the pot and using metal tongs to turn them over so they are evenly golden brown, 1 to 2 minutes total. Use tongs to remove the long johns, and drain on a paper towel–lined plate. Cool, then dip one side into the vanilla glaze.

chocolate cake donuts

My son, John, begged me for a long time to make an allergy-friendly chocolate cake donut just like the ones his siblings have eaten at Dunkin' Donuts, and here it is. What I love most about this donut is that it is very easy to make, has no rise time, and no crazy list of ingredients. Just mix and fry!

MAKES 10 DONUTS

1¾ to 2 cups unbleached all-purpose flour or gluten-free flour blend

⅓ cup unsweetened cocoa powder

½ cup sugar

1 teaspoon baking soda

1 teaspoon baking powder

¾ teaspoon salt

¾ cup soy or rice milk

1 tablespoon water

2 tablespoons vegetable or canola oil

1½ teaspoons vanilla extract

Vegetable or canola oil for frying

CHOCOLATE GLAZE

1 cup allergy-friendly chocolate chips or chocolate pieces

❋ In the bowl of an electric mixer fitted with the paddle attachment, combine 1¾ cups of the flour, the cocoa powder, sugar, baking soda, baking powder, and salt using a wire whisk.

❋ In a small saucepan, combine the soy milk, water, oil, and vanilla and heat over low heat until warmed through. Add the warmed milk mixture to the bowl of the mixer and mix until a soft dough is formed, adding up to an additional ¼ cup flour if necessary.

✳ Turn the dough out onto a lightly floured surface and roll out ½ inch thick. Use a donut cutter dipped in flour to cut out donut shapes. Alternatively, if you don't have a donut cutter, use a 2- to 3-inch biscuit cutter to cut circles, and use a smaller cutter, such as a pastry bag tip, to cut smaller circles in the center.

✳ Heat 3 to 4 inches of oil in a Dutch oven or heavy pot to 380°F. Use metal tongs to carefully place 2 or 3 donuts into the hot oil, one at a time. Fry for 1 to 2 minutes on each side, until the donuts float to the top and are lightly browned. Remove with tongs to a plate lined with paper towels and let cool slightly while you make the glaze.

✳ **TO MAKE THE GLAZE,** heat the chocolate in a microwave-safe bowl for 20 to 30 seconds, until just half of the chips are melted. Use a rubber spatula to mix until everything is melted. Alternatively, place the chocolate chips in a small saucepan and stir over very low heat, using a rubber spatula, until the chips are melted, 2 to 3 minutes. Dip the tops of the donuts into the glaze and let set for 2 to 3 minutes before serving.

chocolate chip cinnamon rolls

This recipe is a delicious variation of my original Cinnamon Roll recipe, found at www.foodallergymama.com. It is truly special, and perfect for holiday mornings when the pace is a little slower. The beauty of these rolls is that they can be prepared the night before and popped in the fridge until the next morning, when you're ready to bake them.

SERVES 6

1 cup soy or rice milk

¼ cup sugar

¼ cup dairy-free shortening

1 teaspoon salt

3½ cups unbleached all-purpose flour or gluten-free flour blend

One .25-ounce package active dry yeast

2 tablespoons vanilla extract

FILLING

¼ cup dairy-free margarine, melted

½ cup sugar mixed with 2 teaspoons ground cinnamon

1 cup allergy-friendly mini chocolate chips

DAIRY-FREE CREAM CHEESE FROSTING

1 cup confectioners' sugar

½ cup dairy-free cream cheese

¼ cup dairy-free margarine

1 tablespoon vanilla extract

❊ In a small saucepan, combine the soy milk, sugar, shortening, and salt and heat over low heat until just warm, about 115°F (use an instant-read thermometer). Remove from the heat.

✳ Meanwhile, combine 2 cups of the flour and the yeast in the bowl of an electric mixer fitted with the paddle attachment and add the warmed soy milk mixture. Mix on low speed until incorporated.

✳ Scrape down the sides of the mixer with a rubber spatula and add the vanilla. Mix on high speed for 2 minutes. Add the remaining 1½ cups flour and mix until the dough comes together.

✳ Transfer the dough to a lightly floured surface and knead for about 5 minutes, until the dough is elastic. Place the dough in a bowl coated with dairy-free cooking spray, cover with a clean dish towel, and let rise until doubled in bulk, about 1 hour.

✳ Punch the dough down and divide it in half. On a lightly floured work surface, roll each dough half into an 8 x 12-inch rectangle. Brush each half with melted margarine and sprinkle evenly with the cinnamon-sugar mixture, then top with the chocolate chips.

✳ Starting with the long side, roll the dough halves up and seal the edges with a little bit of water, making sure the seam is sealed tight. Tuck in the edges with your fingers if necessary.

✳ Coat two 9-inch round cake pans with dairy-free cooking spray. Cut each roll into 1-inch slices, and put the slices cut side down into the prepared cake pans. Cover with a dish towel again and let rise for about 30 minutes. Alternatively, cover with plastic wrap and refrigerate overnight. When ready to bake the next morning, leave the dough on the counter for 15 minutes while the oven is preheating.

✳ During the final rise, preheat the oven to 375°F.

❊ Place the rolls in the oven and bake for 18 to 20 minutes, until lightly browned.

❊ While the rolls are in the oven, make the cream cheese frosting by combining all the ingredients until creamy.

❊ While the rolls are still warm, spread the cream cheese frosting over the top. The rolls are best eaten the day they're made.

hot cross buns

I love to serve these adorable little buns for brunch on Easter Sunday.

MAKES 16 BUNS

3½ to 4 cups unbleached all-purpose flour or gluten-free flour blend

Two .25-ounce packages active dry yeast

1 teaspoon ground cinnamon

¼ teaspoon ground nutmeg

½ teaspoon salt

¾ cup dairy-free buttermilk (see page 6)

½ cup vegetable or canola oil

⅓ packed cup light brown sugar

3 tablespoons water

⅔ cup currants or raisins

ICING

1 cup confectioners' sugar

1 to 1½ tablespoons soy or rice milk

1 teaspoon vanilla extract

✳ In the bowl of an electric mixer fitted with the dough hook attachment, combine 2 cups of the flour, the yeast, cinnamon, nutmeg, and salt.

✳ In a medium saucepan, combine the buttermilk, oil, brown sugar, and water and heat over low heat until the mixture reaches 110 to 115°F as tested with an instant-read thermometer (a minute or 2). Add the buttermilk mixture to the mixer bowl and mix on low speed for 1 minute, scraping the dough from the sides so it is evenly incorporated. Slowly add the remaining flour, ½ cup at a time, until the dough is soft and pliable. Use a rubber spatula to stir in the currants.

❋ Place the dough in a bowl coated with dairy-free cooking spray. Cover with a dish towel and let rise for 1 to 1½ hours, until doubled in bulk. Punch down, cover again, and let rest for 10 minutes. Divide the dough into 16 pieces and form them into smooth balls. Place on a baking sheet lined with parchment paper, spacing them 1 inch apart. Cover with a dish towel again and let rise for 30 to 45 minutes, until the dough has risen slightly more.

❋ Meanwhile, preheat the oven to 375°F. At this point you can either cut a cross into the top of each dough ball, using a sharp paring knife, or simply put dough in the oven. Bake for 13 to 15 minutes, until light golden brown.

❋ Mix the icing ingredients together in a small bowl, using enough soy milk so the mixture is easy to drizzle. Let the buns cool slightly on a wire rack and pipe the icing mixture over the cut portion of the dough or pipe the icing into a cross pattern.

3

✳

Having a child with food allergies pretty much guarantees you'll be making lunches every single day for many years. When my son John started to bring his own lunch in first grade, I nearly had a panic attack. First, I was scared of him eating lunch around kids who brought peanut butter and jelly sandwiches every day. But also I was terrified to be solely responsible for making him a safe and delicious lunch he would actually eat and not throw out. That's a tall order for any mom, not just those who have food-allergic kiddos.

But over time, I realized that lunch really isn't that big of a deal once you have a few standby recipes that your kids will love. Think outside the "lunch" box and send your child with lunches that are the envy of their friends. And lunch at home should be about sharing a wonderful meal together as a family. Weekends are the perfect time to make homemade soup and sandwiches or special salads. And whatever you do, never forget the lunch-box treat!

fruit kabobs with dairy-free yogurt and granola dip

This is a nice change from the daily lunch-box grind. It's easy, fresh, and healthy and packs well in a resealable plastic container. Use the skewered fruit to "dip" into the yogurt and granola mixture.

SERVES 1

½ cup soy or other dairy-free plain yogurt

¼ cup Healthier Granola (page 34)

Assorted fresh fruit: grapes, whole or halved strawberries, blueberries, melon chunks, papaya chunks, pineapple chunks, mango chunks, Granny Smith apple slices, peach slices, plum slices, nectarine slices

1 wooden skewer, cut in half, or several toothpicks

✳ In a small resealable container, layer half the yogurt, half the granola, and then the remaining yogurt, followed by the remaining granola. Seal tightly and pack with skewers threaded with your favorite fruit.

waldorf salad

The first time I ever tasted Waldorf salad was when I lived on a kibbutz in Israel. One of my jobs was to prepare food for everyone in the kibbutz, which was essentially a small town! One day I helped make the day's meal and had to peel hundreds, and I mean hundreds, of apples for an incredible Waldorf salad. This is a very light and healthy version of that traditional one, and is perfect for little lunch boxes.

SERVES 4

6 Fuji or Gala apples, peeled, cored, and diced

2 stalks celery, thinly sliced

2 cups red or green grapes, or a combination of the two, cut in half before measuring

1 cup raisins, golden raisins, currants, or dried cranberries

1 cup dairy-free yogurt

2 tablespoons vegan mayonnaise

1 tablespoon freshly squeezed lemon juice

Zest of 2 lemons

Kosher salt and freshly ground pepper

✳ In a large bowl, combine the apples, celery, grapes, and raisins. In a small bowl, combine the yogurt, mayonnaise, lemon juice, lemon zest, and salt and pepper to taste. Pour the yogurt mixture over the fruit and stir well. Pack in insulated lunch boxes.

citrus salad with jícama

I first fell in love with citrus salad when I was pregnant with my daughter, Chloe. I was obsessed, and ordered it nearly every day during my lunch break when I worked at WBBM-TV. Unlike most of my other pregnancy cravings, this one stuck with me, and I still enjoy having it for lunch. I love the adaptability of the salad; my kids aren't crazy about red grapefruit, so when I make it for them I just use all navel oranges or even some blood oranges. The jícama provides a nice contrasting crunch.

SERVES 4

1½ cups 1-inch pieces peeled red grapefruit

1½ cups 1-inch pieces peeled navel oranges or blood oranges

1½ cups peeled, diced jícama

Zest and juice of 1 lime

Zest and juice of 1 medium lemon

2 tablespoons extra virgin olive oil

¼ teaspoon dry mustard

Kosher salt and freshly ground pepper

1 tablespoon chopped fresh mint (optional)

✳ Combine the grapefruit, oranges, and jícama in a medium bowl. In a small separate bowl, combine the lime juice and zest, lemon juice and zest, oil, mustard, and salt and pepper to taste. Pour the dressing over the citrus mixture, toss together gently, and add the mint, if using. Serve as is or on a bed of Bibb lettuce leaves.

spinach salad with champagne vinaigrette

My six-year-old, Matthew, actually created this salad by mixing the reds and greens while I whipped up the vinaigrette. It is simple, beautiful, and a perfect salad for the holidays or really every day. I typically make this salad for lunch with leftover roasted chicken, but it can easily be a dinner entrée too.

SERVES 4

6 cups baby spinach

1 cup thinly sliced strawberries

¼ cup pomegranate seeds

1 unpeeled Granny Smith apple, cored and thinly sliced

CHAMPAGNE VINAIGRETTE

¼ cup extra virgin olive oil

3 tablespoons Champagne vinegar

1½ teaspoons Dijon-style mustard

¼ teaspoon kosher salt

Freshly ground pepper

✻ In a medium bowl, combine the spinach, strawberries, pomegranate seeds, and apple, tossing well.

✻ In a small jar or bowl, combine the oil, vinegar, mustard, salt, and pepper to taste and shake or whisk until the oil is emulsified and the ingredients are combined. Drizzle the vinaigrette over the salad, toss, and serve.

classic cobb salad

A crisp and cool Cobb salad is my go-to lunch on hot and lazy summer days. There's no cooking involved, just chopping and assembling. I've even served this dish for dinner when I don't feel like slaving over a hot grill or stove. It's also the perfect bento lunch-box lunch—drizzle the avocado with a little fresh lemon juice to keep it green and fresh until lunchtime.

SERVES 4

1 head romaine lettuce, roughly chopped

1 avocado, peeled, pitted, and diced

2 vine-ripened tomatoes, seeded and diced

6 to 8 slices cooked bacon, roughly chopped

1½ cups diced leftover Weeknight Double Roast Chicken (page 139)

1½ cups diced cooked ham

RED WINE VINAIGRETTE

¼ cup red wine vinegar

¾ cup extra virgin olive oil

1 teaspoon grainy mustard

Kosher salt and freshly ground pepper

❊ Arrange the lettuce on a large platter. Line up the avocado, tomatoes, bacon, chicken, and ham evenly across, forming rows.

❊ In a small measuring cup, whisk together the vinegar, oil, mustard, and salt and pepper to taste. Serve the dressing alongside the salad. The dressing will keep covered in the refrigerator for up to 1 week.

chicken salad

This is my favorite way to use up leftover cooked chicken from my Weeknight Double Roast Chicken. It is very fresh, light, and flavorful. I love to serve it on a bed of spinach salad or tuck it into allergy-friendly pita bread. Feel free to omit the celery, grapes, or apple, or add some raisins according to your personal taste.

SERVES 2

2 cups diced leftover Weeknight Double Roast Chicken (page 76)

¼ cup vegan mayonnaise

¼ cup dairy-free sour cream

½ teaspoon freshly squeezed lemon juice

½ teaspoon Dijon-style mustard

¼ cup finely minced celery

¼ cup finely diced peeled and cored Gala or Granny Smith apple

½ cup coarsely chopped red grapes

Kosher salt and freshly ground pepper to taste

✳ In a medium bowl, combine all the ingredients. Serve as is or in allergy-friendly mini pita bread, tortillas, or your favorite sandwich bread.

broccoli and chicken pasta salad

This is my "carpool crazy sports night" meal, but also my kids' favorite lunch-box pasta salad. Feel free to add other veggies or meats.

SERVES 4

Kosher salt

2 cups allergy-friendly or gluten-free bow-tie pasta or tubular or spiral pasta

2 cups broccoli florets

2 tablespoons extra virgin olive oil

1 cup shredded leftover Weekday Double Roast Chicken (page 76)

Freshly ground pepper

❋ In a large pot of boiling salted water, cook the bow-tie pasta for 8 minutes, then add the broccoli florets. Cook for an additional 3 to 4 minutes, until the pasta is al dente and the broccoli is crisp-tender. Drain and run cool water over the pasta and broccoli mixture to stop the cooking. Drain well and transfer to a large bowl. Toss with the oil, add the chicken, and season with salt and pepper to taste.

eggless egg salad sandwiches

I've loved egg salad sandwiches since I was a kid. It's really easy to make an eggless egg salad sandwich; simply substitute extra-firm tofu for the hard-boiled eggs. This recipe follows my minimalist style of cooking— a little bit of each ingredient goes a long way and tastes fresh. I love to serve this salad tucked into allergy-friendly pita bread along with red lettuce leaves and thinly sliced tomato. My kids like it with toasted bread.

SERVES 4

One 14-ounce package extra-firm tofu, drained and dried with paper towels

½ cup finely diced celery

2 tablespoons vegan mayonnaise

2 tablespoons dairy-free sour cream

2 tablespoons coarse Dijon-style mustard

1 teaspoon freshly squeezed lemon juice

¾ teaspoon kosher salt, plus more to taste

½ teaspoon freshly ground pepper, plus more to taste

½ teaspoon paprika

¾ teaspoon dry mustard

½ teaspoon celery seeds

1 tablespoon dill relish

4 allergy-friendly pitas or 8 slices allergy-friendly bread

Shredded lettuce and tomato slices

✳ Crumble the drained tofu into a medium bowl. Add the celery and lightly stir with a fork.

✻ In a small bowl, combine the mayonnaise, sour cream, Dijon-style mustard, lemon juice, salt, pepper, paprika, dry mustard, celery seed, and relish. Add to the tofu mixture and stir well. Season with salt and pepper to taste. Make sandwiches with the mixture, finishing with lettuce and tomato slices. Serve immediately, or refrigerate the salad and make the sandwiches when you're ready to put together lunch.

honey and "butter" sandwich

This was my favorite sandwich growing up. I never tired of it. Sweet honey and butter slapped in between slices of Wonder Bread equaled perfection. We're all a lot more health conscious now, but with a little updating, this sandwich can and should make an appearance in lunch boxes all over again. Double or triple the recipe as needed.

SERVES 1

2 slices allergy-friendly or gluten-free bread
1 tablespoon dairy-free margarine, softened
1 tablespoon honey
½ banana, sliced (optional)

❋ Lightly toast the bread slices. Spread a layer of margarine and honey on one slice of toast. Top with the banana slices, if using. Top with the second piece of toast, cut in half, and serve.

soy or sunflower butter and banana sandwich

The original may have been Elvis's signature sandwich, but this version is a favorite in my home (and made peanut free). It's my go-to sandwich when the kids have a field trip and need a nonperishable lunch.

SERVES 1

1½ tablespoons soy or sunflower butter

2 slices allergy-friendly or gluten-free bread

½ banana, sliced

✳ Spread the butter on one slice of the bread. Top with the banana slices and the other bread slice and press down lightly. Slice in half and serve.

turkey and dairy-free cheese panini

My son, John, loves grilled panini sandwiches and often requests that I make his sandwiches hot when he's home for lunch on the weekends. You don't actually need a panini maker for this recipe: Make your own sandwich press by placing your sandwich in a skillet or grill pan, then place a heavy skillet or pan holding a large can on top to weight it down. Grill or toast, then flip. You could also use a waffle iron, which the kids will love. This recipe serves one but can easily be doubled, tripled, or quadrupled to feed a larger crowd.

SERVES 1

1 tablespoon dairy-free margarine

2 slices allergy-friendly or gluten-free bread

¼ cup shredded dairy-free cheddar cheese

2 slices smoked turkey

2 thinly sliced vine-ripened tomatoes

1 slice cooked bacon, cut in half (optional)

❋ Heat a grill pan, panini maker, or waffle maker.

❋ Spread the margarine over the slices of bread. Place the cheese, turkey, tomatoes, and bacon, if using, evenly on the side of a bread slice without the margarine. Top with the other bread slice, margarine side facing up, place the sandwich on the grill pan, and fry for about 2 to 3 minutes on each side, or until the cheese is melted and the bread is toasted. (Or cook in a panini maker or waffle maker according to the manufacturer's instructions.)

blt

In the summertime there is nothing better than a beautifully ripened tomato, either from the farmers' market or your own garden. I love fresh tomatoes just sprinkled with a little kosher salt, and they are the shining star in the classic BLT sandwich. On my laziest or busiest night, this is the perfect dinner. Pair it with a crisp romaine salad or soup.

SERVES 4

10 to 12 slices bacon

3 tablespoons dairy-free margarine

8 slices allergy-friendly or gluten-free bread

8 teaspoons Chipotle Mayonnaise (page 22)

2 ripe large tomatoes, cut into thick slices

4 large romaine lettuce leaves

✳ Cook the bacon in a skillet over medium heat for 3 to 4 minutes on each side, until crisp. Drain on paper towels.

✳ Heat a large grill pan over medium-low heat. Spread the margarine evenly over one side of each bread slice and toast the bread on each side until lightly grilled. Spread 1 teaspoon of the mayonnaise over each slice. Divide the cooked bacon slices, tomatoes, and lettuce, among 4 slices of bread, buttered sides up, and top each with the remaining slices to make sandwiches. Cut in half and serve.

turkey meatball hero

This is a fantastic way to use leftovers from my Pasta and Turkey Meatballs recipe. Sometimes I double the recipe so I can have enough leftovers to make sandwiches the next night.

SERVES 4

> **2 cups leftover turkey meatballs and sauce (from Pasta and Turkey Meatballs, page 115)**
>
> **4 allergy-friendly Italian sandwich rolls or gluten-free rolls**
>
> **1 cup shredded dairy-free mozzarella cheese (optional)**

❀ Put the turkey meatball and sauce mixture into a medium saucepan and warm over medium-low heat until heated through. Cut the meatballs in half if you like.

❀ Preheat the broiler and line a baking sheet with foil. Split open the rolls, place them on the prepared baking sheet, and lightly toast under the broiler for about 1 minute. Remove from the broiler and divide the meatballs and sauce evenly among the toasted rolls. Divide the cheese, if using, over the meatballs. Place the sandwiches back under the broiler for a couple of minutes more, until the cheese and sauce are bubbling. Cut in half and serve immediately. The hero can be served open-face or sandwich-style.

french dip sandwiches

French dip sandwiches typically take quite a bit of time to make, but not this version. This is a fantastic lunch to make at home on a chilly winter day. Besides, what kid doesn't love to dip a sandwich?

SERVES 4

SANDWICHES

1½ cups low-sodium beef broth or water

⅓ cup soy sauce (omit for soy allergies)

¼ teaspoon dried thyme

1 medium garlic clove, finely minced

2 tablespoons Worcestershire sauce
(omit for soy allergies)

1 pound allergy-friendly deli roast beef, thinly sliced

4 allergy-friendly or gluten-free hoagie rolls,
toasted

DIPPING SAUCE

1¾ cups low-sodium beef broth

✳ In a medium saucepan, combine the beef broth, soy sauce, thyme, garlic, and Worcestershire sauce, if using. Place over medium heat, bring to a simmer, and simmer for 3 to 4 minutes, then add the roast beef. Simmer for another 3 to 4 minutes, until the meat is heated through.

✳ Meanwhile, pour the broth for the dipping sauce into a small saucepan and place over low heat. Bring to a simmer and simmer for 3 minutes. Add 2 tablespoons of the soy sauce–broth mixture and heat through. Divide the dipping sauce among 4 small bowls. (I like to heat my dipping sauce separately in order to achieve a clear broth, but if you don't want to fuss with an extra pan, just add the broth to the heating liquid after removing the roast beef and use that as your dipping sauce.)

✳ Use tongs to divide the roast beef evenly among the hoagie rolls. Cut in half and serve with bowls of dipping sauce alongside.

meat loaf sandwich

Meat loaf sandwiches for your child's lunch box? Of course! Once I told my boys that eating meat loaf sandwiches was like eating hamburgers, they dug it. Everyone knows that the best part of meat loaf for dinner is the leftover sandwiches the next day. They're learning. . . .

SERVES 1

> 1 tablespoon Chipotle Mayonnaise (page 22) or prepared vegan mayonnaise
>
> 2 thick slices allergy-friendly or gluten-free bread or round rolls, lightly toasted
>
> 1 thick slice leftover Family-Style Meat Loaf (page 148)
>
> 1 thick slice beefsteak tomato
>
> 1 leaf Bibb or red leaf lettuce

✳ Spread the mayonnaise over 1 slice of toasted bread. Layer with the meat loaf, tomato, and lettuce. Top with the second bread slice, cut in half, and serve.

the ultimate sandwich wrap

I hesitate even writing a recipe for a wrap because there are dozens, perhaps hundreds of delicious ways to make them. So I've decided to offer a template of suggestions, ready to be mixed and matched with what you and your kids love. Wraps are the ultimate food to let your kids make on their own. It inspires their creativity in the kitchen and gives them the confidence to start making their own favorite recipes.

SERVES 1

THE BASE

Dairy-free cream cheese, allergy-friendly pesto (see page 23), Chipotle Mayonnaise (page 22), soy butter, Easy Pizza Sauce (page 159)

THE WRAP

Allergy-friendly or gluten-free tortillas, butter lettuce or red lettuce leaves

THE "INNER WORKINGS"

Roasted turkey breast, smoked ham, salami, leftover Weekday Double Roast Chicken (page 139), leftover San Francisco Joe's Special (page 143), leftover Family-Style Fajitas (page 154), Chicken Salad (page 77), Eggless Egg Salad (page 79), turkey salami, shredded dairy-free cheese, shredded carrots, lettuce, cucumber, tomatoes, avocado, corn, salsa, sliced fruit

THE ROLL

✳ Spread a thin layer of base over the tortilla or lettuce leaf. Layer with your choice of "inner workings," and roll the tortilla lengthwise, seam side down. Tuck in the edges and cut the wrap into pinwheel shapes or in half. Wrap in foil and warm in the oven for a hot wrap, parchment for a cool wrap. Pinwheels can be placed in a bento box or other reusable container.

chicken and vegetable quesadillas

This is another way to use up leftover cooked Weeknight Double Roast Chicken. There used to be a great little place under the El tracks in my old neighborhood in Chicago called Texas Star Fajita Bar, and I would always order a delicious spinach and mushroom quesadilla. It was one of my favorite snacks and now it is also my kids' favorite at home.

SERVES 4

1 tablespoon extra virgin olive oil or vegetable oil

½ medium onion, very thinly sliced

2 medium garlic cloves, minced

3 packed cups baby spinach leaves

1½ cups sliced mushrooms

2 cups shredded leftover Weekday Double Roast Chicken (page 139)

1 teaspoon chili powder

½ teaspoon kosher salt

¼ teaspoon freshly ground pepper

Eight 8-inch allergy-friendly or gluten-free tortillas

1½ cups shredded dairy-free Monterey Jack cheese

Salsa, dairy-free sour cream, and chopped cilantro for serving

❊ Preheat the oven to 400°F and line a large baking sheet with foil.

❊ In a large skillet, heat the oil over medium heat. Add the onion and garlic and sauté for 3 to 5 minutes, until the onion is translucent. Add the spinach, mushrooms, chicken, chili powder, salt, and pepper and cook for an additional 5 to 8 minutes, until the mixture is warmed through.

❋ Place 4 tortillas on the prepared baking sheet and divide the filling mixture evenly among them. Sprinkle the shredded cheese over the mixture and top with the remaining tortillas.

❋ Bake for 10 to 12 minutes, until the tortillas are starting to brown and the cheese is melted. Cut into wedges and serve with salsa, sour cream, and cilantro.

mini corndogs

One day my son, John, came home from school bummed out because, he said, every kid in the lunchroom ordered the corndogs from the cafeteria that day. He felt completely left out and slightly embarrassed that he was forced to eat a turkey sandwich. I realized right then and there that we had to make corndogs at home so he could try them for himself. These little corndogs are as good as, if not better, than the ones found at carnivals. The best part is that they freeze really well and can be reheated in a 400°F oven for about 10 minutes.

SERVES 8

1 cup unbleached all-purpose flour or gluten-free flour blend

1 cup cornmeal

4 teaspoons baking powder

½ teaspoon salt

¼ teaspoon freshly ground pepper

¼ teaspoon paprika

1 cup soy or rice milk

¼ cup honey

2 tablespoons water

1 quart vegetable oil for frying

8 wooden skewers, cut in half

8 turkey or beef hot dogs, cut in half

Ketchup and mustard for dipping

❋ **FIRST, MAKE THE BATTER:** Combine the flour, cornmeal, baking powder, salt, pepper, and paprika in a large bowl. In a liquid measuring cup, combine the soy milk, honey, and water using a wire whisk. Add the liquid ingredients to the dry ingredients and stir until just combined. Put the batter in the fridge to set a little, about 5 minutes.

❋ Meanwhile, heat the oil in a large cast-iron pan to 365°F, using a candy thermometer to check the temperature. Stick half a wooden skewer into each hot dog half.

❋ Remove the batter from the fridge; if it's a little thick, swirl a teaspoon or two of water into it. Dip the hot dogs into the batter. Use your hands or a teaspoon to evenly spread and coat the hot dogs, taking care not to overcoat them or the hot dogs won't cook properly when they are fried.

❋ Use metal tongs to carefully place the corndogs into the hot oil; fry, turning as necessary, until all sides are a nice golden brown, about 2 minutes. Remove with metal tongs to a paper towel–lined plate.

❋ Serve with little ramekins of ketchup and mustard or, better yet, mix the two together.

classic mac 'n' cheese

The stovetop portion of this dish takes only twenty minutes start to finish—almost exactly the same amount of time it takes to make that boxed, powdery, fake cheese kind.

SERVES 4

¼ cup dairy-free margarine

¼ cup unbleached all-purpose flour or gluten-free flour blend

1½ cups soy or rice milk, warmed

1 cup shredded dairy-free cheddar cheese

1¼ teaspoons kosher salt

¼ teaspoon freshly ground pepper

½ teaspoon dry mustard

½ pound cooked elbow macaroni

✳ In a medium saucepan, melt the margarine over medium-low heat. Add the flour and whisk for 1 minute. Add 1 cup of the warmed soy milk and whisk constantly for 3 minutes, or until the mixture is thickened and coats the back of the spoon. Add the cheese and stir with a wooden spoon for about 5 minutes, until melted. Add the remaining ½ cup warmed milk, the salt, pepper, dry mustard, and macaroni. Stir until the cheese sauce is incorporated and smooth. Add the macaroni, stir, and serve.

4

✳

Soups are perfect for lunch or dinner, or even in between. They are a fast, healthy, and economical way to use up leftovers in a warm and satisfying meal, but they're also great to freeze for a rainy day.

I love to bring over soups to new moms, sick relatives, or even friends who just need some extra help for dinner. The best part about soups is that they are a wonderful way for kids to get involved in the kitchen to make their own versions or recipes. There really is no wrong way to make soup—just chop, simmer, and serve!

soups

easy chicken pasta soup

This is the soup I make when my kids are sick or a friend is under the weather. It's simple and comforting in every way.

SERVES 4

One 48-ounce box low-sodium chicken broth

¼ cup finely chopped yellow onion

¼ cup finely chopped celery

¼ cup finely chopped carrot

1 cup allergy-friendly or gluten-free small pasta

1½ cups diced or shredded leftover Weekday Double Roast Chicken (page 139)

Kosher salt and freshly ground pepper

1 tablespoon chopped fresh flat-leaf parsley (optional)

✳ Pour the chicken broth into a Dutch oven or soup pot and bring to a simmer over medium heat. Add the onion, celery, and carrot and simmer for about 10 minutes. Add the pasta and cook for an additional 8 to 10 minutes, depending on the size of the pasta and the suggested cooking time on the package. Add the chicken and simmer for 2 minutes more. Season with salt and pepper to taste. Sprinkle the parsley on top, if using, and serve.

chicken tortilla soup

This is a hearty and fresh-tasting soup that everyone loves. I like to crush allergy-friendly tortilla chips at the bottom of each bowl and pour the soup directly over the chips. It's spiced on the mild side for little kids, but if you like a spicier soup, add an additional ½ teaspoon or more chili powder and ground cumin, along with some hot sauce on top.

SERVES 4

1 tablespoon extra virgin olive oil

1 medium onion, diced

3 small garlic cloves, minced

1½ teaspoons chili powder

½ teaspoon ground cumin

1 teaspoon kosher salt

½ teaspoon freshly ground pepper

One 28-ounce can diced tomatoes, with juices

One 32-ounce box low-sodium chicken broth

1½ cups fresh or frozen (unthawed) corn

2 packed cups baby spinach

2 cups shredded leftover Weekday Double Roast Chicken (page 139)

Juice of 1 lime

2½ cups allergy-friendly or gluten-free tortilla chips, broken into pieces

SOUP TOPPINGS

Chopped fresh cilantro

Lime slices

Sliced green onions

Dairy-free sour cream

Hot sauce

✳ In a large soup pot or Dutch oven, heat the oil over medium-high heat. Add the onion and garlic and sauté for 5 to 7 minutes, until the onion is softened. Add the chili powder, cumin, salt, and pepper and cook for an additional 1 to 2 minutes, until the spices are fragrant. Add the diced tomatoes and chicken broth and simmer for 10 minutes. Add the corn, spinach, chicken, and lime juice. Give the pot a stir and simmer for an additional 5 minutes, or until the soup is slightly thickened.

✳ Place about ¼ cup broken tortilla chips into each bowl and ladle the soup over the chips. Top with any or all of the suggested toppings.

french onion soup

One of my favorite dishes to order at restaurants is a bubbling hot French onion soup. I love to make this dairy-free version at home because it's both easy and economical. Your kids will love the gooey dairy-free cheese on top.

SERVES 6

¼ cup dairy-free margarine

8 cups thinly sliced onions

1 garlic clove, minced

½ teaspoon dried thyme

1 teaspoon kosher salt

½ teaspoon freshly ground pepper

1 bay leaf

½ cup dry red wine

2 tablespoons unbleached all-purpose flour or gluten-free flour blend

One 48-ounce box low-sodium beef broth

1 allergy-friendly or gluten-free baguette, sliced ½ inch thick

1 cup shredded dairy-free mozzarella cheese

❋ In a large Dutch oven, melt the margarine over medium heat. Add the onions, garlic, thyme, salt, pepper, and bay leaf and sauté for 20 to 25 minutes, stirring often, until the onions are a deep golden color and caramelized. Add the flour and stir to combine. Add the wine, scraping up the browned bits at the bottom of the pot. Cook, stirring, until the wine is evaporated, then add the beef broth. Bring to a boil, then reduce the heat and simmer for 15 minutes, or until the broth is slightly thickened. Remove the bay leaf.

❋ While the soup is simmering, preheat the broiler to high. Place the bread slices on a baking sheet and toast under the broiler for 2 to 3 minutes, until lightly toasted. Remove the baking sheet from the oven, but leave the broiler on.

✻ Divide the soup evenly among ovenproof soup bowls. Place 1 or 2 slices of toasted bread on top of the hot broth, sprinkle with cheese, and place bowls on the baking sheet. Broil for 1 to 2 minutes, until the cheese is bubbling and starting to brown. Serve immediately; bowls will be very hot.

MAKE-AHEAD TIP • The soup can be made a day in advance, cooled to room temperature, and refrigerated in an airtight container. Reheat gently on the stovetop, then continue with the bread and shredded cheese portion of the recipe.

creamy tomato soup

Grilled cheese and tomato soup go together like peas and carrots. And kids love to dip their favorite sandwiches into a hot and creamy bowl of soup like this one. This is the easiest and most delicious tomato soup you'll ever make, and it freezes well. The best part of this soup is that it is so much healthier than traditional cream of tomato soup, as it doesn't have any cream in it—but it tastes like it does! It's perfect to send in your kid's thermos for lunch.

SERVES 4

2 tablespoons dairy-free margarine

1 tablespoon extra virgin olive oil

½ cup diced yellow onion

½ cup diced celery

½ cup diced carrot

1 garlic clove, minced

1 teaspoon dried basil, or 2 to 3 roughly chopped fresh basil leaves

½ teaspoon dried thyme

½ teaspoon kosher salt, plus more to taste

¼ teaspoon freshly ground pepper, plus more to taste

⅛ teaspoon ground cloves

2½ tablespoons unbleached all-purpose flour or gluten-free flour blend

One 28-ounce can diced tomatoes

2⅔ cups low-sodium chicken broth

¼ cup tomato paste

❊ In a Dutch oven or soup pot, heat the margarine and oil over medium heat. Add the onion, celery, carrot, garlic, basil, thyme, salt, pepper, and cloves and sauté for 5 minutes, or until the onion is softened. Add the flour and cook for 1 minute. Add the diced tomatoes, chicken broth, and tomato paste and give the pot a few stirs to incorporate the ingredients. Bring to a simmer, then reduce the heat to low and simmer for 20 minutes, or until the soup is thickened and the flavors are combined.

✻ Use an immersion blender or standard blender to blend the soup until smooth and creamy. Taste and season with additional salt and pepper if needed.

FREEZER TIP • The soup can be frozen in 2-cup portions in freezer bags or reusable containers for up to 2 months.

butternut squash soup

This is one of my favorite soups to serve during the holidays. Lightly toasted croutons are delicious perched right on top of the soup for a nice contrast in texture.

SERVES 4

1 large butternut squash, peeled, seeded, and cut into 1-inch cubes

1 medium yellow onion, cut into 1-inch cubes

1 yellow potato, peeled and cut into 1-inch cubes

1 teaspoon kosher salt, plus more to taste

½ teaspoon dried thyme, or leaves from 2 to 3 sprigs of fresh thyme

½ teaspoon freshly ground pepper, plus more to taste

2 tablespoons extra virgin olive oil

One 32-ounce box low-sodium chicken broth, warmed

CROUTONS

¼ cup vegetable or canola oil

½ loaf allergy-friendly or gluten-free bread, cut into 1-inch cubes

❋ Preheat the oven to 425°F.

❋ Combine the squash, onion, potato, salt, thyme, and pepper on a large rimmed baking sheet. Toss with the 2 tablespoons oil and bake for 30 to 40 minutes, or until vegetables are softened and beginning to brown.

❋ **MEANWHILE, MAKE THE CROUTONS:** Heat the oil in a medium skillet over medium-high heat. Add the bread cubes and cook for 5 to 10 minutes, stirring, until toasted and browned on all sides. Remove and drain on a plate lined with paper towels.

✳ Bring the chicken broth to a simmer in a large soup pot.

✳ Add the roasted vegetables to the soup pot and puree using an immersion blender. Alternatively, puree in batches in a regular blender or food processor. Season with salt and pepper to taste and top each bowl with croutons.

FREEZER TIP • The soup can be frozen in 2-cup portions in freezer bags or reusable containers for up to 2 months.

creamy broccoli and potato soup

I used to love to make this soup with lots of butter and cheese. Of course, that was back in the day when I didn't know much about food allergies. This version is exactly like the original, creamy and delicious but without any dairy at all. It is a sturdy soup that could easily be dinner on its own with a green salad and crusty allergy-friendly bread.

SERVES 4

2 tablespoons extra virgin olive oil

2 tablespoons dairy-free margarine

1 small onion, diced

2 medium garlic cloves, finely minced

1½ pounds broccoli, cut into florets

4 to 5 medium russet potatoes, peeled and diced

1¾ teaspoons kosher salt, plus more to taste

½ teaspoon freshly ground pepper, plus more to taste

One 32-ounce box low-sodium chicken or vegetable broth

3 tablespoons chopped fresh dill

❊ In a large Dutch oven or heavy soup pot, heat the oil with the margarine. Add the onion, garlic, broccoli, potatoes, salt, and pepper and sauté for 8 to 10 minutes, until the vegetables are softened. Add the broth, bring to a boil, then reduce the heat, cover, and simmer for 25 to 30 minutes, stirring occasionally and using the back of a wooden spoon to break up some of the potatoes. Add the dill and season with additional salt and pepper if needed. Serve immediately.

simple vegetable soup

This is my go-to soup all year long when I want to use up veggies in the fridge or if I need a fast and soothing veggie side dish. The key to making this soup quickly is to dice and dump as you go along. Once you cut the onion, throw it in the pot. As the onion is sautéing, add the carrot, let it sauté while you cut the celery, and so on. Feel free to add or omit any veggies according to your family's taste.

SERVES 4

2 tablespoons dairy-free margarine

2 tablespoons extra virgin olive oil

1 small onion, diced

2 carrots, diced

2 celery stalks, diced

2 russet or red potatoes, peeled and diced

2 medium zucchini, diced

1 cup diced green beans

1 cup sliced kale leaves

8 cups low-sodium chicken broth

½ teaspoon kosher salt

¼ teaspoon freshly ground pepper

1 bay leaf

½ teaspoon celery seeds

❋ In a large soup pot or Dutch oven, heat the margarine and olive oil. Add the onion and sauté for 2 minutes. Add the carrots and sauté for 2 minutes, add the celery and sauté for 2 minutes, add the potatoes and sauté for 2 minutes, add the zucchini and sauté for 2 minutes, add the green beans and sauté for 2 minutes; add the kale and sauté for a final 2 minutes.

✳ Add the broth, salt, pepper, bay leaf, and celery seeds. Give the soup a stir, cover the pot halfway, and simmer for 45 minutes to 1 hour. Season with additional salt and pepper to taste. Remove the bay leaf before serving.

FREEZER TIP • The soup can be frozen in 2-cup portions in freezer bags or reusable containers for up to 2 months.

tomato, chicken, and gnocchi soup

I've been making this soup for years. It's my daughter Chloe's all-time favorite dinner, and she requests it for her birthday every year. Feel free to use allergen-friendly packaged gnocchi or homemade gnocchi. In a pinch I love to use allergy-friendly small pasta in place of the gnocchi.

SERVES 4

2 tablespoons dairy-free margarine

2 small garlic cloves, finely minced

One 32-ounce box low-sodium chicken broth

1 17-ounce package allergy-friendly gnocchi, or 2 cups homemade Potato Gnocchi (page 126)

One 14.5-ounce can diced tomatoes, with juices

2 cups baby spinach leaves

2 cups shredded leftover Weekday Double Roast Chicken (page 139)

5 or 6 basil leaves, roughly chopped or torn, or ½ teaspoon dried basil

Kosher salt and freshly ground pepper

Grated dairy-free Parmesan cheese for topping

❋ Heat the margarine in a soup pot or Dutch oven over medium heat. Add the garlic and cook until fragrant, about 1 minute. Add the chicken broth and bring to a boil. Reduce the heat to low and add the gnocchi. Simmer for 3 to 4 minutes. (If using frozen gnocchi, no need to thaw. Just put them right into the simmering soup and cook until they float to the top.) Add the tomatoes, spinach, chicken, and basil and season with salt and pepper to taste. Ladle into bowls and serve with grated Parmesan cheese on top.

carrot soup

This is another delicious and healthy soup with a short ingredient list. It freezes well and is a great addition to any lunch box.

SERVES 4

15 medium carrots, cut into 1-inch pieces

1 large sweet onion, cut into 1-inch pieces

3 garlic cloves, peeled and smashed

2 tablespoons extra virgin olive oil

1½ teaspoons kosher salt, plus more to taste

¼ teaspoon freshly ground pepper, plus more to taste

¼ teaspoon dried thyme

One 32-ounce box low-sodium chicken broth

Freshly grated nutmeg for sprinkling

❋ Preheat the oven to 400°F.

❋ Combine the carrots, onion, garlic, oil, salt, pepper, and thyme on a baking sheet and spread the vegetables out in an even layer. Roast for about 40 minutes, until the vegetables are lightly browned and softened.

❋ While the vegetables are roasting, bring the chicken broth to a simmer in a soup pot. Add the roasted vegetables to the broth and puree using an immersion blender. Or puree in batches using a regular blender or food processor. Season with salt and pepper to taste and top each bowl with a little nutmeg.

FREEZER TIP • The soup can be frozen in 2-cup portions in freezer bags or reusable containers for up to 2 months.

5

❊

"What's for dinner, Mom?" I hear that question every day of my life. And believe me, there are times when I am so tired and wish I could just do a drive-through dinner or pick up the phone and order a pizza. But when you have a family that lives with food allergies, this isn't possible. So it's important to have a game plan in place for the week so you're never caught off guard with nothing to feed your family.

I always tell my readers to try not to get intimidated by complicated dinner recipes. And definitely don't overthink your meal; sometimes you will have only twenty minutes together for a meal because of busy schedules, and that's good enough. For busy nights, do something easy like spaghetti with garlic oil, or if you have more time, especially on weekends, make a comforting roasted chicken dinner with all the trimmings. Better yet, make two roasted chickens so you'll have leftovers during the week. Dinner is an important meal, not just because we're all hungry but because it's a wonderful way to slow down, relax, and connect with those you love.

spaghetti with garlic oil

If you have nothing to make for dinner, try this. It is the dinner I turn to when I have close to nothing in the fridge or pantry, have only ten minutes to make dinner, and want to serve something that I know every single one of my kids will eat. The parsley is optional; my kids prefer this dish without a trace of anything green.

SERVES 6

¼ cup extra virgin olive oil

2 garlic cloves, finely minced to a paste (see Note)

One 16-ounce package allergy-friendly or gluten-free spaghetti

Kosher salt and freshly ground pepper

¼ cup roughly chopped fresh flat-leaf parsley (optional)

Grated dairy-free Parmesan cheese for sprinkling (optional)

❋ Heat the oil in a large sauté pan or skillet over low heat. Add the garlic and season with pepper and heat over very low heat, making sure not to brown or burn the garlic.

❋ Meanwhile, cook the pasta according to the package directions. Drain, add it to the garlic oil, and toss to coat evenly. Season with salt and pepper to taste, add the parsley, if using, toss, and serve immediately, with Parmesan cheese if you like.

NOTE • To mince the garlic into a paste, combine it with about ⅛ teaspoon kosher salt and mash it with the back of your chef's knife, rocking it back and forth until a paste is formed.

pesto pasta with green beans and potatoes

I used to make pesto pasta all the time before I had John; it was my husband's favorite pasta sauce. Of course, the traditional version contains pine nuts and cheese, so I had to figure out a way to make an allergy-friendly version that was safe and delicious. This is it, and it's served as a very traditional Italian dish, pasta with boiled green beans and potatoes. Be sure to reserve a little of the pasta cooking water to thin out the sauce when adding it to the pasta.

SERVES 4

PESTO

2 packed cups fresh basil leaves

½ cup extra virgin olive oil

2 medium garlic cloves, chopped

½ teaspoon kosher salt

¼ teaspoon freshly ground pepper

2 tablespoons dairy-free margarine, softened

⅓ cup grated dairy-free Parmesan cheese

PASTA WITH GREEN BEANS AND POTATOES

One 16-ounce package allergy-friendly or gluten-free spaghetti or penne pasta

5 small new potatoes, peeled and cut in half

2 cups fresh green beans, trimmed

Grated dairy-free Parmesan cheese for topping (optional)

❋ **TO MAKE THE PESTO,** in a food processor or blender, combine the basil, oil, garlic, salt, and pepper and puree. Pour the mixture into a bowl and stir in the softened margarine and Parmesan cheese.

❋ Cook the pasta according to the manufacturer's directions; drain, reserving ½ cup of the pasta cooking water. Transfer to a large bowl.

❋ Meanwhile, fill a medium saucepan halfway with water, put a cover on it, and bring it to a boil. Add the potatoes and cook just until one can be pierced with a fork, 10 to 15 minutes, depending on the size of the potato. Remove the potatoes using a slotted spoon and place them in the bowl with the pasta. Add the green beans to the boiling water and cook for 5 minutes, or until tender but still al dente. Remove the beans using a slotted spoon and add them to the bowl with the potatoes.

❋ Add just enough of the pasta cooking water to the pesto to make it a little creamier, then add the pesto mixture to the pasta mixture. Stir gently until combined. Serve topped with additional grated Parmesan cheese if you like.

pasta and turkey meatballs

Spaghetti and meatballs are a classic kid's dinner. It's also one of my most requested recipes at www.foodallergymama.com. I can get this dinner on the table in less than thirty minutes, yet it tastes like it simmered all day long. The best part is that the leftover sauce and meatballs can be turned into a fantastic Turkey Meatball Hero (page 85).

SERVES 4

MEATBALLS

1 pound dark meat ground turkey (do not use extra-lean)

¾ cup panko crumbs (you may use gluten-free panko or bread crumbs)

1 teaspoon dried Italian seasoning

¼ teaspoon dried thyme

½ teaspoon kosher salt

¼ teaspoon freshly ground pepper

2 tablespoons water

SAUCE

1 tablespoon extra virgin olive oil

1 small onion, grated

1 cup grated veggies (I like a combination of carrots and zucchini; omit if your kids aren't thrilled with the veggies)

1¾ teaspoons dried Italian seasoning

¼ teaspoon dried thyme

Kosher salt and freshly ground pepper

One 28-ounce can crushed tomatoes

One 15-ounce can tomato sauce

1 tablespoon minced fresh flat-leaf parsley (optional)

1 tablespoon minced fresh basil (optional)

One 16-ounce package allergy-friendly or gluten-free pasta

Garlic Bread (page 26) for serving

❋ Preheat the oven to 425°F and line a baking sheet with parchment paper.

❋ In a large bowl, combine all the meatball ingredients well. Use your hands to roll the mixture into 1-inch balls and place them on the parchment paper. Bake for 15 minutes, or until no longer pink on the inside. Set aside.

❋ Meanwhile, heat a large Dutch oven or heavy pot over medium-high heat for about 1 minute. Add the oil and the onion and/or veggies to the pot. Add the Italian seasoning, thyme, and salt and pepper to taste and sauté for 5 minutes, or until the onion is translucent. Add the tomatoes and tomato sauce, bring to a simmer, then reduce the heat to low and simmer for 15 minutes. Stir in the parsley and basil, if using.

❋ Bring a large pot of water to a boil, add salt, and cook the pasta according to the package directions. When the meatballs come out of the oven, add them to the sauce and simmer for 5 additional minutes. Drain the pasta and pour it into a large bowl; add the meatballs and sauce. Serve with garlic bread and a salad on the side.

baked ziti

There are a million recipes out there for baked ziti, and everyone seems to have their own version of baked pasta with cheese. When I want a baked pasta dish, I don't want something that resembles lasagna. Instead, I want something that I can make in less than thirty minutes and doesn't require a lot of ingredients. Feel free to change the ingredients according to whatever you have in the house.

SERVES 6

One 16-ounce package allergy-friendly or gluten-free ziti or rigatoni

2 tablespoons extra virgin olive oil

¼ cup finely diced onion

1 pound ground turkey or beef

2 medium garlic cloves, minced

One 28-ounce can crushed tomatoes

1 teaspoon kosher salt

½ teaspoon freshly ground pepper

½ teaspoon dried thyme

4 tablespoons grated dairy-free Parmesan cheese

One 10-ounce package dairy-free mozzarella cheese, shredded

❋ Cook the pasta according to the package directions; drain and place in a large bowl.

❋ Meanwhile, heat the oil in a large skillet over medium-high heat. Add the onion and sauté until softened, 3 to 4 minutes. Add the ground turkey and cook for 8 to 10 minutes, until no longer pink and cooked through. Add the garlic, stir, and cook for about 1 minute, until the garlic is fragrant. Drain the fat from the meat and return the pan to the stove. Add the crushed tomatoes, salt, pepper, and thyme and simmer for about 10 minutes, until heated through and the flavors are combined.

✤ While the sauce is simmering, preheat the broiler to high and lightly coat a 9 x 13-inch baking dish with dairy-free cooking spray.

✤ Add the sauce and 2 tablespoons of the Parmesan cheese to the pasta. Stir well and pour into the prepared baking dish. Top with the shredded mozzarella cheese and the remaining 2 tablespoons Parmesan cheese. Place under the broiler and broil for 3 to 4 minutes, keeping a watchful eye to make sure the cheese melts and gets a little browned but doesn't burn. Remove from the broiler and let stand for 5 minutes before serving.

The granolas found in most grocery stores often contain nuts and are packed with oil and sugar. This one is easily adaptable to whatever you and your family like.

My kids love this dish with toast. It's super-healthy and can be made with any variation of veggies. It also doubles as the perfect "breakfast for dinner" entrée.

Tofu and Veggie Scramble Page 38

An egg, dairy, and nut-free French toast that everyone will enjoy.

Classic French Toast Page 39

Little chocolate wonder waffles that are
perfect for Valentine's Day, for birthday
breakfast-in-bed celebrations, or just to
coax your kids out of bed in the morning.

Double Chocolate Waffles   Page 47

Here is Matthew, devouring
a chocolate chip muffin.

Double Chocolate Chip Muffins   Page 52

Who wouldn't want delicious and healthy
Morning Glory Muffins (Page 50) for breakfast?

The perfect cake to serve in the
fall, when apples are plentiful.

Spiced Apple Bundt Cake   Page 56

This takes only twenty minutes start to finish and tastes twenty times better than the boxed kind.

Classic Mac 'n' Cheese   Page 94

The easiest and most delicious tomato soup you'll ever make, with the perfect side, cornbread.

Creamy Tomato Soup and **Baked Cornbread**   Pages 101, 179

This is my go-to soup all year long
when I want to use up veggies.

Simple Vegetable Soup   Page 106

Nut and dairy-free Pesto Pasta
with Green Beans and Potatoes (Page 113),
an updated version of an Italian classic.

Two of my kids' favorite lunch-box meals. **Broccoli and Chicken Pasta Salad** (Page 78) and **French Onion Dip** (Page 20) with vegetables, in my favorite Allergy Apparel and Grand Trunk lunch boxes.

My daughter, Chloe, enjoying mealtime.

ir in 1/4 c. flour, cook 2
utes, stirring continuously. Pour
hot chicken stock, bit by bit,
time, stirring well. Add defrosted
een beans

mmer 20 minutes uncovered.

nwhile make Dumplings:

n flour, salt, baking powder in
bowl. Add egg, milk & herbs,
necessary cook, add mixture to
ry mixture & stir in a spatula
l dough just comes together.

e for chicken. Use a rounded
poon to scoop balls of batter
on top sauce. It should cover
on top. Cover & cook 15-20
s until firm. Season to salt
ipe.

350° then 375
1 hour   45 minutes
1 hour

DOUBLE this
2 lbs.

Meat loaf

1 T. extra virgin olive oil
1 carrot, peeled & minced
1 celery stalk, minced
1/2 medium onion, minced + 1/4 c. mushroom
1 garlic clove, minced   mince
1 3/4 tsp. kosher salt
1/8 tsp. pepper
1/4 c. chicken broth
1 T. Ketchup
2 T. Water
1 lb. ground sirloin or chuck + 1/2 c.
pan
Topping: (3/4 c. Dijon
1/2 c. Ketchup
1 T. Store Ground Mustard   mix in
1 tsp. brown sugar   bowl
1/8 tsp. dry mustard

1. Preheat oven to 375 degrees & line
pan sheet w/ foil
2. Heat olive oil in medium skillet. Add
carrot, celery, onion, garlic, mushroom
Add 3/4 tsp. kosher salt, pepper. Sauté
12 minutes or until softened. Add 1/4 c.
broth, 1 T. ketchup & 2 T. water. Mix well

A family meal book in the making . . .

This is one of my most requested recipes at www.foodallergymama.com.
I can get this dinner on the table in less than thirty minutes,
yet it tastes like it simmered all day long.

Pasta and Turkey Meatballs   Page 115

MealtImes can always create
special memories for
the whole family.
My sons Michael (left) and
John and Matthew (below).

Every mom should have a good slow-cooker recipe that's easy and that can cook itself on a lazy Sunday afternoon or during the week while the kids are at school.

Slow-Cooker Italian Beef   Page 165

Delicious **Chicken Salad** (Page 77) with allergy-friendly pita chips is perfect for lunch boxes, for kids and grown-ups alike!

One of our favorite weekday dinners
and my son John's request for
his birthday dinner.

Turkey Sloppy Joes   Page 144

Freckles and Sloppy Joes.

What's not to like?

This is the epitome of sugar
and spice and everything nice.
My kids love this cookie as a
sweet after-school snack.

Sugar and Spice Cookies   Page 188

These stay fresh for a few days, making
them the perfect treat to bake ahead
of time. I've made them for holidays
and birthdays, and as teacher gifts.

Chocolate Crinkles   Page 194

I wanted to re-create the magic of Little Debbie snacks for my son John, and all my other kids, who never get to have any Little Debbie treats in our house. It is one of my all-time favorite recipes, and I promise it will be one of yours too.

Oatmeal Crème Pies   Page 200

Michael and David enjoying their treats.

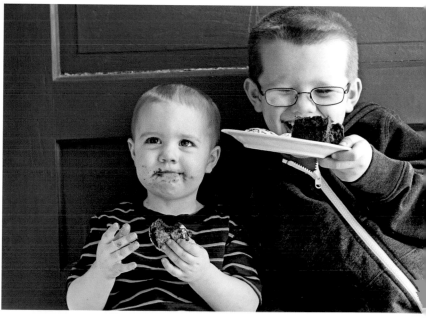

classic lasagna

For people with dairy and egg allergies, lasagna generally is taboo. It took many years to create something as good as the lasagna I grew up loving; this is the result, and it's healthier and much lighter than standard lasagna.

SERVES 6

TOMATO SAUCE

1 teaspoon extra virgin olive oil

1 pound ground turkey (not lean)

Kosher salt and freshly ground pepper

One 24-ounce jar marinara sauce or 2 cups homemade sauce (see page 115)

¼ cup chopped fresh basil

¼ cup chopped fresh flat-leaf parsley

DAIRY-FREE BÉCHAMEL SAUCE

¼ cup dairy-free margarine

3 tablespoons unbleached all-purpose flour or gluten-free flour blend

2 cups dairy-free soy or rice milk

⅛ teaspoon ground nutmeg

Kosher salt and freshly ground pepper

DAIRY-FREE SPINACH RICOTTA

Two 15-ounce packages firm tofu (undrained)

¾ teaspoon agave nectar or honey

1½ tablespoons apple cider vinegar

1½ teaspoons kosher salt

¼ teaspoon freshly ground pepper

One 10-ounce package frozen chopped spinach, thawed, thoroughly squeezed, and drained

½ 10-ounce package no-boil allergy-friendly or gluten-free lasagna noodles

2 cups shredded dairy-free mozzarella cheese

✲ Preheat the oven to 400°F and coat the bottom of two 8-inch square glass baking dishes with margarine. (Alternatively, use a 9 x 13-inch glass baking dish. I prefer to make 2 smaller lasagnas, one for now, one to freeze for later.)

✲ **TO MAKE THE TOMATO SAUCE,** heat the oil in a large skillet over medium-high heat. Add the ground turkey, add a pinch of salt, and a few grinds of pepper and cook until the turkey is no longer pink and is cooked through. Add the marinara sauce, basil, and parsley. Bring to a simmer, then reduce the heat to low and start making the béchamel sauce.

✲ **TO MAKE THE BÉCHAMEL SAUCE,** melt the margarine in a small saucepan over low heat. Add the flour and whisk until the flour is incorporated and not lumpy, about 1 minute. Slowly add the soy milk, and then add the nutmeg, and the salt and pepper to taste. Whisk constantly for 10 to 15 minutes, until the mixture resembles heavy cream and coats the back of a wooden spoon. Add the béchamel sauce to the tomato sauce and stir to combine and heat through. (The béchamel sauce is added directly to the tomato sauce to give it a creamier, cheesy consistency, which is especially important when using dairy-free cheese.)

✲ **TO MAKE THE SPINACH RICOTTA,** mix all the ingredients in a medium bowl.

✲ **START LAYERING:** Ladle ¼ cup of the sauce into each prepared pan. Add the lasagna noodles, layer one-third of the ricotta mixture on top of the noodles, then a layer of sauce, then ¼ cup shredded mozzarella cheese. Repeat 2 times, ending with the sauce on top. Cover tightly with foil. (You can freeze one lasagna pan at this point; see below. Reserve any leftover cheese for another use.) Bake for 45 minutes, up to an hour for a 9 x 13-inch dish. Remove the foil and sprinkle ¼ cup mozzarella cheese on top. Switch the oven to broil and broil for about 2 minutes, until the cheese is lightly browned.

❋ Remove from the broiler, let the dish stand for 10 minutes, cut into squares, and serve.

❋ To freeze for later: Line the unbaked lasagna with plastic wrap, then cover with aluminium foil. Freeze for up to 2 months.

stuffed shells

I often call stuffed shells "lazy mom's lasagna." The ingredients are similar but prepared in a fraction of the time. It can easily be made in advance earlier in the day and heated through later, or frozen for up to two months. I love to use homemade tomato sauce, but any allergy-friendly store-bought marinara sauce would be great too.

SERVES 4

One 10-ounce package allergy-friendly or gluten-free jumbo pasta shells

One 15-ounce package extra-firm tofu, drained and crumbled

1 teaspoon apple cider vinegar

½ teaspoon agave nectar

¾ teaspoon kosher salt

½ teaspoon freshly ground pepper

One 10-ounce package frozen spinach, thawed, thoroughly squeezed, and drained

¼ cup dairy-free grated Parmesan cheese

4 cups tomato sauce (see page 115) or jarred marinara sauce

1½ cups shredded dairy-free mozzarella cheese

❋ Preheat the oven to 350°F. Cook the shells according to the package directions for al dente; drain.

❋ In a medium bowl, combine the tofu, vinegar, agave nectar, salt, pepper, spinach, and Parmesan cheese. Ladle 2 cups of the tomato sauce into the bottom of a 9 x 13-inch broiler-safe casserole dish. Use a teaspoon to distribute the tofu mixture evenly into the cooked shells. Place the stuffed shells in the casserole dish and pour the remaining 2 cups tomato sauce over the top of the shells. Cover with a layer of parchment paper, then a layer of foil, and bake for 30 minutes, or until the sauce is bubbling.

❋ Turn the broiler on. Uncover the shells, sprinkle the mozzarella cheese on top, and broil for 2 to 3 minutes, until the cheese is melted and lightly golden. Remove from the oven and let sit for 5 to 10 minutes before serving.

grandma rudnicki's bolognese sauce

My children lovingly refer to this sauce as Grandma's Meat Sauce and often request it to be made for their special birthday dinners at home. In fact, my mother-in-law always made this sauce during the holidays on December 23, to celebrate her grown children's birthdays (and those of her daughters-in-law). She served it with a delicious homemade ravioli, but we serve it with easy allergy-friendly pasta. I also love to serve it with homemade Potato Gnocchi (page 126). The best part is that it literally makes itself as it simmers on the stove for hours, ready for dinner when you are. This sauce freezes well too.

SERVES 6

¼ cup extra virgin olive oil

2 stalks celery, chopped

2 carrots, chopped

1 medium onion, diced

2 large garlic cloves, minced

2 tablespoons chopped fresh flat-leaf parsley, or
2 teaspoons dried parsley

1 pound ground pork

1 pound ground beef (I love ground chuck, but if you
want something lower in fat, try ground sirloin)

1 teaspoon ground cinnamon

1 tablespoon kosher salt

Freshly ground pepper

One 6-ounce can tomato paste

6 cups water

✻ Heat the oil in a large Dutch oven over medium-high heat. Add the celery, carrots, and onion and sauté for 5 minutes, or until translucent. Add the garlic and parsley and sauté for 2 minutes. Add the ground pork and beef and break them up with a wooden spoon, cooking until the meat is no longer pink, 6 to 8 minutes. Add the cinnamon, salt, and pepper.

✻ Place the tomato paste in a large bowl and whisk in the water. Add the tomato paste and water mixture to the meat mixture. Bring to a simmer, then reduce the heat to low and simmer for at least 4 hours, up to 5 hours, skimming the fat off the top with a ladle as necessary. The sauce should be quite thick, but if you find it is starting to dry out, add a tablespoon or two of water to thin it out. Serve over allergy-friendly pasta.

FREEZER TIP • Cool the sauce to room temperature and freeze in 2-cup portions in resealable containers or freezer bags for up to 2 months.

potato gnocchi

Gnocchi is actually very easy to make and requires few ingredients. The most important thing to remember is to use a light hand in mixing, kneading, and rolling. These take just seconds to cook and can be added directly to a homemade tomato or Bolognese Sauce (page 124) or my Tomato, Chicken, and Gnocchi Soup (page 108). This recipe can easily be doubled.

SERVES 6

Kosher salt

2 pounds Yukon gold potatoes, peeled and cut in half

2 cups unbleached all-purpose flour or gluten-free flour blend, plus more if needed

2 tablespoons extra virgin olive oil

❋ Line a baking sheet with parchment paper and set aside.

❋ Bring a large pot of salted water to a boil. Add the potatoes and cook until just tender when pierced with a paring knife, about 15 minutes. Drain well and run the potatoes through a ricer into a large bowl. Cool.

❋ Add the flour, ½ teaspoon salt, and the oil to the potatoes and use clean hands to lightly bring the dough together. Turn the dough out onto a lightly floured surface and divide it into 6 equal portions. The dough should feel smooth and pliable. Roll each portion into a cylinder about 1 inch thick. Use a bench scraper or butter knife to cut the rolls into ½-inch pieces. Hold a kitchen fork parallel to your work surface. Put one piece on the fork, tines facing you, and use your finger to gently press down on the middle of the gnocchi and let it roll gently toward the handle of the fork. Let the gnocchi drop onto the prepared baking sheet. Repeat with the remaining gnocchi.

✤ Bring a large pot of salted water to a boil. Add the gnocchi and cook for 15 to 20 seconds, until the gnocchi pop up to the surface of the water. Use a slotted spoon to remove the cooked gnocchi and place them on a plate. Add the cooked gnocchi directly to a sauce or soup.

FREEZER TIP • Place uncooked gnocchi on a parchment-lined baking sheet in a single layer. Freeze until firm, then transfer the frozen gnocchi to resealable plastic bags to store in the freezer for up to 2 months.

baked calzones

This is another simple but delicious dough recipe from Aunt Della, and it reminds me of my favorite frozen dinner growing up, Hot Pockets. It's an easy dinner that kids love. The dough is also what Aunt Della uses to make her pizza dough. Aunt Della loves to make her calzones with just cheese, pepperoni, and fresh tomato sauce, and that's how my kids like it too. But you can fill your calzones with all types of leftovers—it's a great way to use them up. (I love to use leftover pot roast, chicken, broccoli, and red peppers, for example). Below I've included a small list of filling ideas; feel free to create your own.

SERVES 6

DOUGH

One .25-ounce package active dry yeast

1 cup plus 2 tablespoons warm water (about 115°F)

2½ to 3 cups unbleached all-purpose flour or gluten-free flour blend, plus more if needed

1 teaspoon kosher salt

FILLING

Fresh tomato sauce

Sausage

Turkey pepperoni

Shredded dairy-free mozzarella cheese

Leafy greens such as kale or Swiss chard sautéed with garlic

Leftover grilled or roasted steak or chicken (Weekday Double Roast Chicken, page 139)

Sautéed spinach and mushrooms

Any leftover vegetables

Fresh or dried herbs

✳ **MAKE THE DOUGH:** In a small bowl, dissolve the yeast in 2 tablespoons of the warm water.

✳ In the bowl of an electric mixer fitted with the dough hook attachment, combine the yeast mixture, the remaining 1 cup warm water, 2 cups of the flour, and the salt. Mix well on medium speed. Add an additional ½ cup flour and continue mixing with the mixer, or knead by hand, for about 5 minutes. Knead until the dough is smooth and pliable, adding more flour if the dough is sticky. This is where you need to "feel" your way through the dough.

✳ Coat a medium bowl with dairy-free cooking spray. Place the dough in the bowl, cover with a dish towel, and let rise until doubled in bulk, 45 minutes to 1 hour.

✳ Toward the end of the rise, preheat the oven to 450°F and line a baking sheet with parchment paper.

✳ Divide the dough into 6 equal portions. On a lightly floured surface, roll each portion of dough into a circle about 6 inches. Be sure not to roll the dough too thin or it may tear.

✳ To fill your calzones, spoon ⅔ cup of your desired filling on the lower half of each circle, leaving a little space at the edges. Fillings include but are not limited to dairy-free cheese, turkey pepperoni, veggies, leftover meats, and herbs, if using. To finish, carefully fold the dough in half and seal the edges by crimping them with your fingers or with a fork.

✳ Place the prepared calzones on the prepared baking sheet and bake for 15 to 20 minutes, until golden brown.

FREEZER TIP • Make extra calzones and freeze them for later: Cool the baked calzones completely and double wrap in plastic, then in aluminum foil, and freeze for up to 2 months. To reheat, unwrap and place on a baking sheet in a preheated 325°F oven for about 10 minutes. Remove from the oven and cool about 5 minutes. Or reheat "Hot Pocket" style by unwrapping the calzones and warming them in the microwave for 2 to 3 minutes, until warmed through.

chicken tenders

Chicken tenders are a kid's menu staple. My kids could eat chicken tenders and nuggets for breakfast, lunch, and dinner if we allowed them! The great thing about this recipe is that it is much healthier than anything you'll find in the freezer section of the supermarket and it takes minutes to prepare. Serve for lunch or dinner with your favorite dipping sauce and a side of steamed veggies.

SERVES 4

¾ cup dairy-free buttermilk (see page 6)

3 garlic cloves, chopped

1 teaspoon kosher salt

½ teaspoon freshly ground pepper

1 pound chicken tenders or pieces

1 cup cornflake crumbs, panko crumbs, or gluten-free or other allergy-friendly bread crumbs

2 tablespoons chopped fresh flat-leaf parsley, or 2 teaspoons dried parsley

1 teaspoon dried Italian seasoning

❊ Preheat the oven to 425°F and coat a large baking sheet with dairy-free cooking spray.

❊ Combine the buttermilk, garlic, salt, and pepper in a medium bowl, add the chicken tenders, and marinate for at least 15 minutes (longer is better; they can marinate in the refrigerator for up to 1 day).

❊ In a 9-inch pie plate, combine the crumbs, parsley, and Italian seasoning. Using tongs, lift the chicken tenders from the buttermilk mixture, shaking off

any excess, and coat thoroughly in the crumb mixture. Place the tenders on the prepared baking sheet and bake for 10 minutes. Turn the pieces over, rotate the pan, and bake for an additional 8 to 10 minutes, just until the tenders are cooked through. Serve immediately, with ketchup on the side.

chicken and rice

My youngest son, Michael, is very fond of this dish. He especially loves the broth-and-vegetable-infused rice, and eats plate after plate of it. I love how everything is cooked and served from the same pot.

SERVES 6

1 tablespoon extra virgin olive oil

1 tablespoon dairy-free margarine

3 carrots, diced

3 stalks celery, diced

1 small onion, diced

1 zucchini, diced

½ small butternut squash, peeled, seeded, and diced
(optional; if in season)

1 large garlic clove, minced

Kosher salt and freshly ground pepper

¼ teaspoon dried thyme

¼ teaspoon celery seeds

1¾ cups basmati rice

One 3- to 4-pound package chicken pieces
(such as legs, quarters, breasts)

1½ cups low-sodium chicken broth

❋ Preheat the oven to 400°F.

❋ In a large Dutch oven, heat the oil and margarine over medium-high heat until the margarine is melted. Add the carrots, celery, onion, zucchini, squash, if using, and garlic, and season generously with salt and pepper. Sauté for 5 minutes and stir in the thyme and celery seeds. Stir in the rice and lightly

toast it for 1 to 2 minutes. Turn off the burner and place the chicken pieces on top of the rice and vegetables. Place the Dutch oven in the oven, uncovered, and bake for 20 minutes. Reduce the heat to 350°F and add the chicken broth. Cover the pot and bake for 40 to 45 minutes, until the chicken is no longer pink inside.

chicken and dumpling stew

When I was a kid, my favorite soup in the world was Campbell's Chicken and Dumplings Soup. I always asked my mom for two cans of soup, just so I could have extra dumplings. Even then I knew that a good chicken and dumpling soup is really all about the big, fluffy dumplings sitting on top of a rich and flavorful stew. This stew is easy and fast enough to make during the week.

SERVES 4

STEW

2 tablespoons dairy-free margarine

1 tablespoon extra virgin olive oil

2 carrots, diced

2 parsnips, peeled and diced

2 celery stalks, diced

1 medium onion, diced

1 garlic clove, minced

2 tablespoons chopped fresh dill

2 tablespoons chopped fresh flat-leaf parsley

1 bay leaf

½ teaspoon kosher salt

¼ teaspoon freshly ground pepper

¼ cup unbleached all-purpose flour or gluten-free flour blend

One 32-ounce box low-sodium chicken broth, warmed

1 cup frozen green beans, thawed

2 cups shredded leftover Weekday Double Roast Chicken (page 139)

DUMPLINGS

1 cup unbleached all-purpose flour or gluten-free flour blend

1¾ teaspoons baking powder

½ teaspoon kosher salt

½ cup dairy-free buttermilk (see page 6)

2 tablespoons water

1 tablespoon chopped fresh dill

1 tablespoon chopped fresh flat-leaf parsley

❋ **TO MAKE THE STEW,** in a large Dutch oven or heavy pot, heat the margarine with the oil over medium heat. Add the carrots, parsnips, celery, onion, garlic, dill, parsley, bay leaf, salt, and pepper and sauté for 5 to 10 minutes, until the vegetables are translucent and softened.

❋ Stir in the flour and cook for 1 minute, stirring constantly. Pour in the warmed chicken broth and stir well. Add the green beans, give the pot another stir, and simmer, uncovered, for 20 minutes, or until the stew is thickened.

❋ **MEANWHILE, PREPARE THE DUMPLINGS:** In a medium bowl, combine the flour, baking powder, and salt using a wire whisk. In a small bowl, combine the buttermilk, water, dill, and parsley. Add the liquid mixture to the dry ingredients and stir with a rubber spatula until just combined. The mixture should be thick.

❋ When the stew is thickened, stir in the chicken. Use a cookie scooper to divide the dumpling batter evenly on top of the hot stew. Cover the pot, and simmer for 20 to 30 more minutes, until the dumplings are firm and set. Remove and discard the bay leaf. Serve immediately.

chicken potpie

Chicken potpies are usually filled with heavy cream and very little of the good stuff, like chicken and vegetables. This one is packed with lots of delicious vegetables and tender chicken. It's a family favorite, especially on chilly nights. If you don't have time to make your own pie crust, you can use a prepared allergen-friendly pie crust.

SERVES 6

PIE DOUGH

1 cup unbleached all-purpose flour or gluten-free flour blend

½ teaspoon sugar

¼ teaspoon salt

⅓ cup dairy-free shortening, chilled and cut into 1-inch pieces

3 to 4 tablespoons ice water

FILLING

1 tablespoon extra virgin olive oil

1 tablespoon dairy-free margarine

½ cup diced onion

½ cup diced celery

½ cup diced carrot

½ cup peeled and diced parsnips

1½ cups sliced mushrooms

1 cup frozen green beans, thawed

1 garlic clove, minced

1 cup diced cooked potato

1 teaspoon kosher salt, plus more to taste

Freshly ground pepper

2¼ cups low-sodium chicken broth

½ cup unbleached all-purpose flour or gluten-free flour blend

**2½ cups diced cooked chicken breast or leftover
Weeknight Double Roast Chicken (page 139)**

¼ teaspoon dried thyme

¼ teaspoon celery seeds

¼ cup chopped fresh flat-leaf parsley

✳ To prepare the pie dough, combine the flour, sugar, and salt in the bowl of a food processor and pulse to combine. Add the shortening and pulse just until the mixture resembles small crumbs. Add the ice water, 1 tablespoon at a time, pulsing just until the dough comes together. Transfer to a sheet of plastic wrap. Use the plastic wrap to pull the sides of the dough together, forming a rounded disk. Refrigerate for at least 15 minutes and up to 3 to 4 days.

✳ Preheat the oven to 400°F and spray a 7 x 11-inch casserole dish with dairy-free cooking spray.

✳ Heat the oil and margarine in a large sauté pan over medium heat. Add the onion, celery, carrot, parsnips, mushrooms, green beans, garlic, potato, and salt and pepper to taste. Sauté for 8 to 10 minutes, until the vegetables are softened and fragrant. Pour the broth into a bowl and slowly whisk the flour into the broth. Add the flour and broth mixture to the vegetables, bring to a simmer, and reduce the heat to low. Simmer for 5 to 6 minutes, stirring, until the mixture is thickened. Stir in the cooked chicken, thyme, celery seeds, and parsley, and season with salt and pepper to taste.

✳ Pour the filling into the prepared casserole dish. Take the chilled pie dough out of the refrigerator and roll it out into a 12-inch rectangle. Place the dough over the filling and cut 2 large slits in the middle with a small paring knife. Bake for 30 minutes, or until the filling is starting to bubble and the crust is browned. Remove from the oven and let stand for 5 to 10 minutes before serving.

weeknight double roast chicken

A simple roast chicken is the easiest thing to prepare during the week; season the chicken, pop it into the oven, and leave it alone for an hour. I always make two roast chickens, one for dinner and the other for leftovers. The next night make Chicken and Vegetable Quesadillas (page 90), Chicken Salad (page 77) sandwiches, or Chicken Potpie (page 137). It is the perfect family supper.

SERVES 6, WITH LEFTOVERS

> **Two 4- to 5-pound chickens, giblets removed, rinsed, and patted dry**
> **1 large lemon, pierced with a fork and cut in half**
> **1 large bunch fresh tarragon**
> **2 tablespoons extra virgin olive oil**
> **Kosher salt and freshly ground pepper**

❄ Preheat the oven to 425°F and place a wire rack in a large roasting pan.

❄ Place the chickens on the rack in the roasting pan. Stuff the cavity of each chicken with a lemon half and a half bunch of tarragon. Tie the legs together, rub the outside of each bird with 1 tablespoon oil, and generously season with salt and pepper.

❄ Roast the chickens for 1 to 1½ hours, until an instant-read thermometer inserted into a breast reads 180°F. Let the chicken rest for a few minutes before carving.

roasted pork tenderloin

Pork roast is a great American classic dinner, and it has been updated here, using pork tenderloin. It's delicious and fast to make, and is sure to become a part of your rotation on busy school nights.

SERVES 4

1 tablespoon roughly chopped fresh rosemary

2 garlic cloves, minced

1 tablespoon stone-ground mustard or Dijon-style mustard

½ teaspoon dry mustard

¼ cup extra virgin olive oil

1¼ pounds pork tenderloin, trimmed

Kosher salt and freshly ground pepper

✳ In a medium bowl, whisk together the rosemary, garlic, mustards, and oil. Add the pork tenderloin, season generously with salt and pepper, and toss with the marinade. Cover and refrigerate for at least 1 hour and up to 8 hours.

✳ Preheat the oven to 400°F. Remove the tenderloin from the marinade and place it in a 9 x 13-inch glass baking dish. Roast for 20 to 25 minutes, until an instant-read thermometer placed in the thickest part of the tenderloin registers 160°F. Let the pork rest for 5 minutes before slicing.

family-style pot roast

Every mom should have a good roast recipe that's easy and can cook itself either on a lazy Sunday afternoon or during the week while the kids are at school. It takes only a few minutes of prep and then you can forget about it until suppertime. I love to use the leftover shredded beef for calzones or sandwiches.

SERVES 6

2 teaspoons kosher salt

1 teaspoon freshly ground pepper

1 tablespoon unbleached all-purpose flour or gluten-free flour blend

One 3½-pound chuck roast

2 tablespoons vegetable or canola oil

2 yellow onions, cut into wedges

2 garlic cloves, minced

2 tablespoons Worcestershire sauce (omit for soy allergies)

2 cups low-sodium beef broth

1 cup water

1 teaspoon dried thyme, or 2 sprigs fresh thyme

½ teaspoon dried rosemary, or 1 sprig fresh rosemary

6 to 8 carrots, cut into 1-inch pieces

6 to 8 boiling potatoes, peeled and cut into 1-inch pieces

❋ Preheat the oven to 350°F.

❋ Combine the salt, pepper, and flour in a small bowl and rub it all over the chuck roast.

❋ Heat the oil in a large Dutch oven over medium-high heat. Add the roast and brown it on all sides, about 10 minutes. Add the onions, garlic,

Worcestershire sauce, broth, water, thyme, and rosemary and bring to a simmer. Turn off the heat, cover the pot, and roast in the oven for 2 hours.

❁ Uncover the pot and arrange the carrots and potatoes around the sides of the roast. Cover and return to the oven for another hour.

san francisco joe's special

It's been written that Joe's Special was invented in San Francisco in the 1920s for hungry jazz musicians. It's the epitome of comfort diner food and surprisingly delicious despite its humble ingredient list. Traditionally the beef and spinach mixture is made with eggs, but it's even better with tofu. If you have a soy allergy, feel free to omit the tofu. The mixture can be spiced up with more Tabasco, and mushrooms can be sautéed along with the beef and spinach. I serve this on dairy-free buttered toast or tortillas.

SERVES 4

2 tablespoons extra virgin olive oil

1 tablespoon dairy-free margarine

½ cup diced onion (small pieces)

1 pound ground sirloin

One 10-ounce package frozen spinach, thawed, squeezed, and drained well

½ teaspoon kosher salt

¼ teaspoon freshly ground pepper

3 to 4 dashes Tabasco sauce

1 cup drained and crumbled extra-firm tofu

¼ cup grated dairy-free Parmesan cheese

❈ In a large skillet, heat the oil and margarine over medium heat. Add the onion and sauté until softened, about 5 minutes. Add the ground sirloin and cook until the meat is no longer pink, 5 to 8 minutes. Add the spinach, salt, pepper, and Tabasco sauce. Cook for 1 to 2 minutes, to warm through, then add the tofu and cook for an additional 2 to 3 minutes, until warmed through. Remove from the heat and top with the Parmesan cheese.

❈ Serve right out of the skillet, alongside allergy-friendly or gluten-free toast or warmed tortillas. It also makes a great filling for a lettuce wrap.

turkey sloppy joes

This is one of our favorite weekday dinners, and it's always my son John's request for his birthday dinner. What I like most about this recipe is that it hides a bunch of little veggies in the sauce, and no one ever suspects. The kids just love it! This is also a great recipe to double and freeze leftovers for another night.

SERVES 6

1 tablespoon extra virgin olive oil

1 small yellow onion, finely diced

½ green bell pepper, seeded and finely diced

½ red bell pepper, seeded and finely diced

1 celery stalk, finely diced

1 carrot, finely diced

1 small garlic clove, finely diced

½ teaspoon kosher salt

¼ teaspoon freshly ground pepper

1½ pounds ground turkey (dark meat)

1 packed tablespoon light brown sugar

1 teaspoon dry mustard

One 15-ounce can tomato sauce

⅓ cup ketchup

1 tablespoon tomato paste

1 tablespoon Worcestershire sauce (omit for soy allergies)

6 allergy-friendly or gluten-free hamburger buns, lightly toasted

✳ In a large skillet, heat the oil over medium-high heat. Add the onion, bell peppers, celery, carrot, garlic, salt, and pepper and sauté until the vegetables are softened and the onion is translucent, about 5 minutes. Add the ground turkey and cook, breaking it up with a wooden spoon, until no longer pink and cooked through, 7 to 9 minutes. Add the brown sugar, mustard, tomato sauce, ketchup, tomato paste, and Worcestershire sauce, stir well, and simmer until slightly thickened, 5 to 7 minutes. Serve on the toasted buns.

FREEZER TIP • The mixture can be frozen for up to 2 months in either a resealable plastic freezer bag or freezer container. Reheat over medium-low heat on the stovetop.

shepherd's pie

This dish is perfect for a cold winter's night. Use leftover mashed potatoes or prepare the mashed potatoes along with the meat mixture. The entire dish is a breeze to put together and makes delicious leftovers.

SERVES 6

1 tablespoon extra virgin olive oil

1 medium onion, diced

4 carrots, diced

2 medium garlic cloves, minced

1 teaspoon kosher salt

½ teaspoon freshly ground pepper

¼ teaspoon dried thyme

1 pound ground sirloin or ground dark turkey meat

2 tablespoons unbleached all-purpose flour or cornstarch

½ cup low-sodium chicken broth

¼ cup ketchup

1½ tablespoons Worcestershire sauce (omit for soy allergies)

1 cup frozen green beans, defrosted

3 cups Creamy Mashed Potatoes (page 170)

½ teaspoon paprika

❋ Preheat the oven to 450°F.

❋ Heat the oil over medium heat in a 10-inch skillet. Add the onion, carrots, garlic, salt, pepper, and thyme. Sauté for 8 to 10 minutes, until the onion is translucent and softened. Add the ground meat and cook until no longer pink, an additional 8 to 10 minutes. Stir in the flour and cook for 1 minute. Add the broth, ketchup, Worcestershire sauce, and green beans. Give it a good stir, cover, and simmer for about 5 minutes, until the mixture is thickened.

❋ Pour the mixture into a 9-inch pie plate or 6 individual ramekins and top with the mashed potatoes. Use a fork to fluff the mashed potatoes and sprinkle the paprika on top. Bake for about 20 minutes, until the pie is heated through and the topping is lightly browned. Serve immediately.

family-style meat loaf

Meat loaf is one of those recipes that just must be in every mom's recipe box. It is easy, filling, and the ultimate comfort food. It also makes fantastic sandwiches the next day. (See page 88 for my favorite meat loaf sandwich recipe.) My version can be made with either ground beef or ground turkey; if you choose ground turkey, be sure to use dark meat.

SERVES 6

1 tablespoon extra virgin olive oil

1 small onion, finely diced

1 medium carrot, finely diced

1 celery stalk, finely diced

¼ cup finely diced mushrooms

2 small garlic cloves, minced

1 teaspoon kosher salt

¼ teaspoon freshly ground pepper

½ cup low-sodium chicken broth

1 tablespoon ketchup

¾ cup allergy-friendly panko crumbs or gluten-free bread crumbs

2 tablespoons water

2 pounds ground sirloin or ground turkey

TOPPING

½ cup ketchup

1 tablespoon stone-ground mustard

1 packed teaspoon light brown sugar

⅛ teaspoon dry mustard

❀ Preheat the oven to 350°F and coat a 9 x 13-inch baking dish with dairy-free cooking spray.

✳ In a 10-inch skillet, heat the oil over medium heat. Add the onion, carrot, celery, mushrooms, garlic, salt, and pepper and cook for 5 to 7 minutes, until the vegetables soften. Add the chicken broth and ketchup and stir well. Cool slightly.

✳ In a medium bowl, combine the panko and water. Add the panko to the vegetable mixture and stir well. Add the ground meat and mix everything together with either your cleaned hands or a fork. Use a light hand and don't overmix.

✳ Turn the meat loaf mixture onto the prepared baking dish and shape into a freeform loaf.

✳ In a small bowl, combine all the topping ingredients and brush the mixture over the meat loaf. Bake for about 1 hour, until an instant-read thermometer inserted into the middle registers 160°F. Let the meat loaf rest for about 5 minutes before serving.

beef stroganoff

This is an update on a traditional family classic. Typically beef stroganoff is served with egg noodles, but we often serve it with rice, white or brown. Feel free to omit the mushrooms if your kids aren't crazy about them. All I know is every single one of my kids loves this dinner, which is saying a lot!

SERVES 4

2 tablespoons dairy-free margarine

1 tablespoon vegetable or canola oil

1¾ pounds top-round steak or tenderloin, cut into ¼-inch-thick slices (make sure the meat is thin and evenly sliced so it cooks quickly and evenly)

¼ cup finely diced onion

3 cups sliced white button mushrooms

1 cup low-sodium beef broth

1 cup dairy-free sour cream

1 teaspoon kosher salt

½ teaspoon freshly ground pepper

⅛ teaspoon freshly grated nutmeg

1 tablespoon snipped fresh chives or minced fresh flat-leaf parsley

4 cups hot cooked white or brown rice

❋ In a large skillet, heat the margarine and oil over medium-high heat. Brown the beef in batches (be sure not to overcrowd the pan), 2 to 3 minutes, transferring it to a plate as it's browned. Once all the beef is browned and on the plate, add the onion to the skillet and sauté for 2 to 3 minutes. Add the mushrooms and cook for an additional 5 minutes, stirring occasionally and scraping up the browned bits from the bottom of the pan, until the mushrooms are softened.

✿ Add the beef broth, continuing to scrape up the browned bits from the bottom of the pan. Whisk in the sour cream until it's incorporated. Return the beef to the pan, reduce the heat to low, add the salt, pepper, and nutmeg, and simmer for 10 minutes, or until the mixture is heated through and slightly thickened. Turn off the heat, sprinkle with the chives, and serve over the rice.

easiest stir-fry

The great thing about stir-fry is that it is completely adaptable to what you have in your kitchen and what your family likes. Add more veggies, less meat, tofu, or just veggies. Have everything chopped up and ready to go before you start to cook and dinner will be done in just a few minutes.

SERVES 4

1 tablespoon cornstarch

1 pound skirt, flank, or boneless sirloin steak, thinly sliced

Juice and zest of 1 orange

1½ tablespoons soy sauce (omit for soy allergies)

3 garlic cloves, minced

¼ teaspoon red pepper flakes

¼ teaspoon paprika

½ teaspoon kosher salt

½ teaspoon peeled, grated ginger

2 tablespoons canola or vegetable oil, plus more if needed

1 bunch asparagus, tough ends trimmed and cut into 1-inch pieces

1 bunch broccoli, cut into small florets

1 cup sliced mushrooms

½ red bell pepper, seeded and thinly sliced

4 cups hot cooked brown or white rice

❋ Sprinkle the cornstarch over the meat and toss to coat evenly.

❋ In a small bowl, whisk together the orange juice and zest, soy sauce, garlic, red pepper flakes, paprika, salt, and ginger, and set aside while you prepare the steak.

✳ In a large skillet, heat 1 tablespoon of the oil over medium-high heat. Add the steak in batches and brown each batch for 2 to 3 minutes, until cooked through. Don't overcrowd the pan, and add more oil as needed. When the last batch of steak is done, add 1 tablespoon oil to the empty skillet. Add the asparagus, broccoli, mushrooms, and bell pepper, give it a good stir, and cook for another 2 to 3 minutes, until the vegetables are crisp-tender.

✳ Add the orange juice–soy sauce mixture and return the beef to the pan. Heat for an additional 1 to 2 minutes to combine the flavors. Serve immediately over the rice.

family-style fajitas

The steak can marinate all day in the fridge and is quickly grilled on an outdoor grill or grill pan. It's an easy, fast, and healthy supper.

SERVES 6

¼ cup extra virgin olive oil

Juice of 2 limes

½ teaspoon lime zest

1 large garlic clove, minced

1 teaspoon ground cumin

1 teaspoon dried oregano

1 teaspoon kosher salt

½ teaspoon freshly ground pepper

1½ pounds flank steak

2 red bell peppers, seeded and thinly sliced

1 green bell pepper, seeded and thinly sliced

½ sweet onion, thinly sliced

6 allergy-friendly or gluten-free tortillas, warmed (see Note)

Dairy-free sour cream for topping

Salsa (either homemade or allergy-friendly store-bought) for topping

❋ In a small bowl, whisk together the oil, lime juice, zest, minced garlic, cumin, oregano, salt, and pepper. Reserve 2 tablespoons of the marinade in a medium bowl.

❋ Combine the steak and marinade in a resealable plastic bag, turning the bag to evenly distribute the marinade. Marinate for at least 1 hour, and up to 6 hours, in the refrigerator. Add the peppers and onions to the reserved marinade and marinate at room temperature for 1 hour.

✳ Heat a ridged grilled pan over medium-high heat, add the meat, and grill for 3 to 4 minutes on each side for medium-rare. Transfer to a cutting board and let the meat stand.

✳ Add the marinated peppers and onion to the hot grill pan and cook until they are crisp-tender and beginning to brown, 3 to 4 minutes.

✳ Thinly slice the meat and serve with the peppers and onions on a platter with the warmed tortillas, sour cream, and salsa alongside.

NOTE • To warm the tortillas, wrap them in paper towels, place on a plate, and microwave for about 45 seconds.

beef taco bar

There's not one kid I know who doesn't love to make his or her own tacos.
It's the easiest dinner to make during the week, and it's also a great kid-friendly
party meal.

SERVES 6

MEAT FILLING

2 tablespoons vegetable or canola oil

1 medium onion, finely diced

2 garlic cloves, minced

2 pounds ground sirloin

2 teaspoons ground cumin

2 teaspoons chili powder

2 teaspoons dried oregano

1½ teaspoons kosher salt

½ teaspoon freshly ground pepper

½ cup water

2 tablespoons tomato paste

TACO BAR FILLING

Shredded lettuce

Diced tomato

Diced avocado

Shredded dairy-free cheddar cheese

Shredded dairy-free sour cream

Prepared salsa

Twelve 6-inch allergy-friendly or gluten-free tortillas,
warmed (see Note)

✳ **TO MAKE THE MEAT FILLING,** in a large skillet, heat the oil over medium heat. Add the onion and garlic and sauté for 5 minutes, or until the onion is softened. Add the ground sirloin and cook for 8 to 10 minutes, until the meat is cooked through and no longer pink. Drain the excess fat. Return the pan to the stove, lower the heat to medium-low, and add the cumin, chili powder, oregano, salt, pepper, water, and tomato paste. Simmer, uncovered, for an additional 5 to 7 minutes, until the mixture has thickened slightly.

✳ Arrange the taco toppings in small serving bowls and put the tortillas on a platter. Have each person make his or her own tacos with the fillings of their choice.

NOTE • To warm the tortillas, wrap them in paper towels, place on a plate, and microwave for about 45 seconds.

make-your-own pizza bar

Families who live with food allergies typically can't have pizza night unless they make their own at home. But honestly, homemade is so much better, healthier, and more fun to make together. It's also a great way to celebrate your kids' birthday parties—just put out a bunch of allergy-friendly toppings and let everyone create their own masterpiece!

quick pizza dough

This dough is the epitome of fast and easy; no rise time needed, and it can even be made ahead of time and refrigerated for up to twelve hours. It also freezes well for up to two months.

MAKES ONE 14-INCH ROUND PIZZA OR 6 MINI PIZZAS

One .25-ounce package active dry yeast

1 cup warm water (110 to 115°F)

2 tablespoons extra virgin olive oil

1 teaspoon sugar

1 teaspoon kosher salt

2½ cups unbleached all-purpose flour, plus more for rolling and kneading

Easy Pizza Sauce (recipe follows)

Pizza toppings (list follows)

❋ Preheat the oven to 450°F and line a baking sheet with parchment paper.

❋ In a small bowl, whisk together the yeast, warm water, and oil.

✳ Combine the sugar, salt, and flour in the bowl of an electric mixer fitted with the dough hook. Add the yeast mixture to the flour mixture and mix on medium speed to combine the ingredients, then increase the speed to high for 1 to 2 minutes, until the dough forms into a ball. If the dough is still a little sticky, add a few additional tablespoons of flour.

✳ Turn the dough onto a lightly floured surface and knead 10 to 15 times, until the dough is smooth and pliable. Roll and stretch into a 14-inch circle or into mini pizzas. Place on the prepared baking sheet, top with pizza sauce and your desired toppings, and bake for 10 minutes, or until the crust is lightly browned on the edges, and the cheese, if using, is bubbling.

easy pizza sauce

I remember like it was yesterday when I tried to make my homemade pizza for the first time, knowing I could never order one again for my family. I looked high and low for jarred pizza sauce that was safe for John, and never found it. It was a blessing in disguise, though, because those limitations opened my eyes to making a fresher, healthier sauce. This sauce is so delicious that my kids will dip a spoon in and eat it straight out of the pot. Easy and yummy!

1 tablespoon extra virgin olive oil

1 medium garlic clove, minced

One 28-ounce can crushed tomatoes

¾ teaspoon dried basil

¾ teaspoon dried oregano

¼ teaspoon dried thyme

¾ teaspoon kosher salt

¼ teaspoon freshly ground pepper

※ Heat the oil over medium heat and add the garlic. Sauté for about 1 minute, until the garlic is fragrant. Add the crushed tomatoes, basil, oregano, thyme, salt, and pepper. Give the pot a good stir and simmer for 20 minutes. Use immediately or freeze for up to 2 months.

pizza toppings

After the kids roll out their pieces of dough, now comes the fun part: spreading homemade sauce and topping with everything they love on their pizzas. Here are just a few ideas to get you started—the sky's the limit!

- Shredded dairy-free mozzarella cheese
- Turkey pepperoni
- Cooked turkey sausage
- Red, green, yellow, and orange bell pepper slices
- Small broccoli florets
- Yellow and red cherry tomatoes, cut in half
- Mushroom slices
- Pitted black or green olives
- Zucchini or yellow squash slices
- Baby spinach leaves
- Chopped Canadian bacon
- Prosciutto slices
- Shredded cooked chicken

baked potato bar

On one particularly busy night, I had nothing to serve for dinner but potatoes and leftovers. Mention "We're having leftovers" to your kids and I promise they'll whine and run the other way. Turning dinner into a make-your-own baked potato activity was pure magic. The kids loved creating their own toppings—and we used up those leftovers too!

SERVES 4

4 large russet potatoes or 4 large sweet potatoes, scrubbed and pricked all over with a fork

✻ Preheat the oven to 400°F.

✻ Place the potatoes directly onto an oven rack and bake for about 45 minutes, until a knife can pierce through the flesh easily.

✻ Remove the potatoes from the oven and make an X shape with a sharp paring knife in the middle of the potato. Use your hands to gently push each side to expose the flesh.

✻ Set out a platter of cooked potatoes and little bowls of assorted toppings for the "bar."

baked potato toppings

- Cooked shredded roasted chicken
- Cooked leftover steak
- Cubed smoked deli ham
- Shredded dairy-free cheddar or Monterey jack cheese
- Steamed fresh broccoli florets
- Diced seeded plum tomatoes
- Crumbled cooked turkey bacon
- Leftover Tofu and Veggie Scramble (page 38)
- Your favorite prepared salsa
- Dairy-free sour cream
- Dairy-free margarine
- Any other leftover veggies or meat you have in the fridge

slow-cooker beef stew

Beef stew is the perfect all-in-one dinner. The thing I love about the slow cooker is that it makes dishes like this a snap to assemble and it's ready for dinner whenever you are.

SERVES 4

1 tablespoon extra virgin olive oil

1 medium yellow onion, diced

2 celery stalks, diced

2 medium carrots, diced

2 medium parsnips, peeled and diced

2 unpeeled yellow potatoes, diced

2 small garlic cloves, minced

1 teaspoon dried thyme

1 bay leaf

1 teaspoon kosher salt

A few grinds of freshly cracked pepper

One 28-ounce can crushed tomatoes

¾ cup water

2½ pounds beef stew meat

✻ In a large skillet, heat the oil over medium-low heat. Add the onion, celery, carrots, parsnips, potatoes, garlic, thyme, bay leaf, salt, and pepper and sauté until softened and the onion is translucent. Pour the vegetable mixture into a 6-quart slow cooker and add the crushed tomatoes, water, and beef. Stir and cook on high heat for 6 hours. Serve as is or with brown rice.

slow-cooker italian beef

This unbelievably simple and delicious recipe comes from my sister, Chris. She always makes it on Halloween night, and it's waiting for the kids when they get home from trick-or-treating. It's also the perfect meal for busy weekday nights.

SERVES 4

3 pounds chuck roast

3 garlic cloves, peeled and smashed

2 teaspoons dried Italian seasoning

1 teaspoon kosher salt

½ teaspoon freshly ground pepper

1 dried bay leaf

One 32-ounce box low-sodium beef broth

Allergy-friendly or gluten-free hoagie rolls, toasted

✳ Place the chuck roast in a 6-quart slow cooker. Sprinkle in the smashed garlic, Italian seasoning, salt, pepper, and bay leaf. Pour the beef broth over the beef and cook on high for 6 hours or low for 8 hours.

✳ Remove the meat from the broth, trim the fat, and shred it, using 2 forks. Return the shredded meat to the broth and stir. Remove and discard the bay leaf. Serve on toasted hoagie rolls with extra broth on the side.

slow-cooker turkey chili

My son, John, is allergic to legumes, so we add extra vegetables in place of beans in this chili. It's fantastic with my Baked Cornbread (page 179).

SERVES 6

2 tablespoons extra virgin olive oil

1 medium onion, diced

1 garlic clove, minced

½ red bell pepper, seeded and diced

½ green bell pepper, seeded and diced

2 pounds dark meat ground turkey

One 28-ounce can diced tomatoes

One 15-ounce can tomato sauce

2 tablespoons tomato paste

2 tablespoons chili powder

1¾ teaspoons ground cumin

¼ teaspoon paprika

¾ teaspoon kosher salt

¼ teaspoon freshly ground pepper

Pinch cayenne pepper (optional)

2 cups frozen corn (unthawed)

Allergy-friendly or gluten-free saltine crackers, cornbread, or tortilla chips for serving

Dairy-free sour cream for serving

Hot sauce for serving (optional)

❋ In a large skillet, heat the oil over medium heat. Add the onion, garlic, and green and red peppers and sauté for 5 minutes, or until the vegetables are beginning to soften. Add the ground turkey and cook until no longer pink and cooked through, 5 to 10 minutes more.

✳ Transfer the mixture to a 6-quart slow cooker. Add the diced tomatoes, tomato sauce, tomato paste, chili powder, cumin, paprika, salt, pepper, and cayenne, if using. Stir, cover, and cook on high for 6 hours. Stir in the frozen corn, lower the setting to warm, and leave for 10 minutes to heat through. Serve with saltine crackers, cornbread, or tortilla chips, and sour cream and hot sauce, if you like.

sides

creamy mashed potatoes

There are many ways to make great mashed potatoes, but this is the basic recipe I use time and again for its simplicity and versatility. I love to use it as a topping for my Shepherd's Pie (page 146), and it is a staple at my holiday table. You can even make it ahead of time, spoon it into a greased 2-quart baking dish, cover with foil, and put in the fridge up to a day in advance. Heat, covered, for about 30 minutes in a preheated 375ºF oven.

SERVES 4

2½ to 3 pounds medium russet, Yukon gold, or red-skinned potatoes, peeled and cut into 1-inch pieces

1 cup dairy-free sour cream

¼ cup dairy-free margarine

1 teaspoon kosher salt, plus more if needed

½ teaspoon freshly ground pepper, plus more if needed

❋ Put the potatoes in a large pot, add water to cover by 1 inch, and bring to a boil. Reduce the heat and simmer for about 20 minutes, until the potatoes are easily pierced with a fork. Drain.

❋ Place the potatoes in the bowl of an electric mixer fitted with the paddle attachment. Add the sour cream, margarine, salt, and pepper and mix on medium speed until the ingredients are combined. Taste and add more salt or pepper if needed.

roasted sweet potato wedges

Billy Dec's Rockit Bar & Grill in Chicago is known for its insanely delish sweet potato fries, and I've been known to eat an entire basket by myself. These wedges are inspired by Billy and Rockit and those incredible fries. I like to serve my sweet potato wedges exactly the way Rockit does, with a side of Chipotle Mayonnaise (page 22).

SERVES 4

3 to 4 large sweet potatoes, peeled and cut into ½-inch wedges
2 tablespoons extra virgin olive oil
2 packed teaspoons light brown sugar
½ teaspoon ground cinnamon

❋ Preheat the oven to 400°F and line a large baking sheet with parchment paper.

❋ Place the sweet potato wedges on the baking sheet, drizzle with the oil, and sprinkle with the brown sugar and cinnamon. Use clean hands to toss together, and roast for 25 to 30 minutes, turning halfway through. Remove from the oven and serve.

roasted root vegetables

Any of your favorite root vegetables can be swapped for the ones below. Even the herbs can be swapped for whatever you have on hand. If you don't happen to have fresh herbs on hand, use 1 teaspoon dried herbs. If you don't have any dried herbs, kosher salt and pepper will still get the job done deliciously.

SERVES 4

2 cups 1-inch pieces carrot

2 cups 1-inch pieces peeled parsnip

4 cups 1-inch pieces unpeeled Red Bliss or Yukon gold potato

2 tablespoons extra virgin olive oil

2 to 3 garlic cloves, peeled and smashed

3 sprigs fresh rosemary

1 teaspoon kosher salt

½ teaspoon freshly ground pepper

❋ Preheat the oven to 400°F.

❋ Place the carrots, parsnips, and potatoes on a large baking sheet. Use two if necessary in order to avoid overcrowding the pan. Drizzle the vegetables with the oil and add the garlic, rosemary, salt, and pepper. Use clean hands to toss everything together right on the baking sheet.

❋ Roast for 25 to 30 minutes, stirring the vegetables once. Serve immediately, or cool and serve at room temperature.

LEFTOVER TIP: Roasted Vegetable Soup

❋ Make a double batch of vegetables, and reserve half to make a delicious soup: Combine the vegetables with about 1½ cups hot vegetable or chicken broth and blend with an immersion blender or a regular blender until smooth.

roasted cauliflower

Sometimes the best preparations are the simplest. Cauliflower has a lackluster reputation, but I promise that once you try my simple roasted version, you'll want to make it again and again. It's easy, fast, and delish!

SERVES 4

1 large head or 2 small heads cauliflower, broken into florets

2 tablespoons extra virgin olive oil

1 teaspoon kosher salt

½ teaspoon freshly ground pepper

2 large garlic cloves, peeled and smashed

½ teaspoon dried thyme

❋ Preheat the oven to 450°F.

❋ Place the cauliflower florets on a large baking sheet. Drizzle with the oil and sprinkle with the salt, pepper, garlic, and thyme. Use clean hands to toss everything together, and roast for 15 to 20 minutes, turning the vegetables once, or until softened and slightly browned. Serve immediately or cool and serve at room temperature.

grilled asparagus

Asparagus is a sure hit among kids. My kids love it simply grilled with just a little salt and pepper. It's my go-to vegetable during the week.

SERVES 4

1 pound asparagus, woody ends trimmed

1 tablespoon extra virgin olive oil

1 teaspoon kosher salt

½ teaspoon coarsely ground pepper

✳ Preheat a stovetop grill or outdoor grill over medium-high heat.

✳ Place the asparagus on a baking sheet and drizzle with the oil. Add the salt and pepper and use your clean hands to toss together. Transfer the asparagus to the grill and cook for 4 to 5 minutes, until lightly charred but still crisp-tender. Serve immediately or cool and serve at room temperature.

sautéed swiss chard

I love the colors of Swiss chard, especially rainbow Swiss chard. It's a beautiful and healthy side dish, and one I promise your kids won't turn their noses at. My kids are somewhat veggie-averse but still love this one.

SERVES 4

2 tablespoons extra virgin olive oil

2 pounds green or rainbow Swiss chard, roughly chopped

2 small garlic cloves, minced

Kosher salt and freshly ground pepper

❈ Heat the oil in a large skillet over medium heat. Add the chard and sauté for 2 minutes. Add the garlic and sauté for another 3 minutes, until the chard is wilted and the stalks are slightly softened. Season to taste with salt and pepper. Serve warm, or cool and serve at room temperature.

simple sautéed corn

During the summer months when corn is in season, I buy as much fresh corn as I can at the farmers' market, cut away the kernels, and freeze them in resealable plastic bags. Frozen corn is fantastic stirred right into soups and chili (such as my Slow-Cooker Turkey Chili, page 166), or simply sautéed with a little dairy-free margarine. It seems so simple, yet it is the best way to serve summer's best produce.

SERVES 4

2 tablespoons dairy-free margarine

Kernels from 7 to 8 ears corn on the cob

½ teaspoon kosher salt, plus more if needed

Freshly ground pepper

½ cup chopped fresh basil (optional)

✳ Melt the margarine in a large skillet over medium-high heat. Add the corn, season with the salt and pepper to taste, and sauté for 10 to 12 minutes, stirring occasionally, until some of the corn kernels turn slightly brown and become caramelized. Remove from the heat, stir in the basil, if using, and season with additional salt and pepper if needed. Serve immediately or cool and serve at room temperature.

everyday stuffing

Many people make stuffing only around the holidays, but for me it's a fast, easy, and inexpensive side dish any time of the year. This stuffing can be made ahead of time, making it a perfect weekday-meal side dish.

SERVES 4

8 cups fresh allergy-friendly or gluten-free bread cubes (cut or torn into 1-inch pieces)

¼ cup dairy-free margarine

¾ cup diced yellow onion

3 stalks celery, diced

1 cup chopped mushrooms

1 teaspoon kosher salt

1¾ teaspoons dried sage

½ teaspoon celery seeds

¼ teaspoon freshly ground pepper

¾ to 1 cup water or low-sodium chicken or vegetable broth

✳ Preheat the oven to 400°F and coat a 7 x 11-inch baking dish with dairy-free cooking spray.

✳ Arrange the bread cubes on 2 baking sheets and toast in the oven for 5 minutes. Transfer to a large bowl and set aside. Reduce the oven temperature to 350°F.

✳ Meanwhile, heat the margarine in a large skillet over medium heat. Add the onion, celery, mushrooms, salt, sage, celery seeds, and pepper and sauté for 5 to 8 minutes, until the vegetables are softened. Transfer the vegetable mixture to the bowl with the bread cubes. Drizzle the water over the mixture, a little at a time, and gently combine with a rubber spatula. The mixture should be moist but not overly soaked.

✳ Transfer the mixture to the prepared baking dish, cover with foil, and bake for 30 minutes. Remove the foil and bake for another 5 to 10 minutes, until the top is lightly browned. (Or if you are preparing the dish ahead of time, cover with foil and refrigerate until ready to bake.) The stuffing can be kept refrigerated for up to 1 day.

baked cornbread

I love it when diners offer cornbread with their soups and salads. It's a perfect match. This cornbread is great with any soup or chili, or even on its own as an afternoon snack. I find that the quality of the cornmeal makes a difference in how tender the cornbread crumb is, so I recommend buying the best organic brand you can. Feel free to omit the frozen corn if you like.

SERVES 6

1 cup unbleached all-purpose flour or gluten-free flour blend

1 cup cornmeal

2¼ tablespoons sugar

1½ tablespoons baking powder

¾ teaspoon baking soda

½ teaspoon salt

1¼ cups dairy-free buttermilk (see page 6)

¼ cup dairy-free margarine, melted

1 cup frozen corn (unthawed; optional)

❋ Preheat the oven to 450°F and line an 8-inch square baking dish with foil, with a 1-inch border hanging over the sides. Coat the foil with dairy-free cooking spray and set aside.

❋ In a medium bowl, combine the flour, cornmeal, sugar, baking powder, baking soda, and salt using a wire whisk. Whisk together the buttermilk and margarine in a liquid measuring cup and add to the dry ingredients. Stir until just combined, then stir in the frozen corn, if using.

✳ Bake uncovered for 20 to 25 minutes, until an inserted toothpick comes out clean and the top is lightly browned. Remove from the oven and let cool for 5 to 10 minutes, then pull the cornbread from the pan using the foil overhang, cool completely, and cut into squares, or fold up and store for later.

baked onion rings

Chicago is home to Portillo's, one of our favorite burger, hot dog, and Italian beef restaurants. We love their fried onion rings, but my food-allergic son John was never able to have one because they are coated in dairy. In fact, John never tried an onion ring until I developed this recipe just for him. My daughter, Chloe, who is a fried-onion-ring expert, says they're awesome, and so does John. These are fantastic with my Chipotle Mayonnaise.

SERVES 4

1 cup dairy-free buttermilk (see page 6)

¼ teaspoon chili powder

¼ teaspoon paprika

1 teaspoon kosher salt

¼ teaspoon freshly ground pepper

¼ cup unbleached all-purpose flour or gluten-free flour blend

1 cup cornflake crumbs or allergy-friendly bread crumbs
(or gluten-free bread crumbs)

3 to 4 large Vidalia onions, cut into thick rings and separated

Ketchup or Chipotle Mayonnaise (page 22)

✽ Preheat the oven to 450°F and coat 2 large baking sheets with dairy-free cooking spray.

✽ In a medium bowl, combine the buttermilk, chili powder, paprika, salt, pepper, and flour. Pour the cornflake crumbs into a 9-inch pie plate. Put the onion rings in the buttermilk mixture. Use a wooden skewer or fork (keeps hands clean and is less messy) to take one onion ring out at a time, allowing any excess buttermilk to drip off, and dip into the cornflake crumbs, coating the surface evenly.

✳ Place the onion rings on the prepared baking sheets, being careful not to overcrowd them. Coat the onion rings lightly with dairy-free cooking spray and bake for 10 minutes. Flip the onion rings and bake for an additional 5 to 10 minutes, until they are crisped and just beginning to brown. Serve immediately with ketchup or chipotle mayonnaise.

6

❊

Ahhh, treats. My favorite thing in the world. My first book, *The Food Allergy Mama's Baking Book,* was pretty much dedicated solely to the world of everything sweet. My friends and readers know I have a wicked sweet tooth that cannot be curbed; I simply must have something sweet every day.

This chapter is filled with a whole bunch of new treats that I'm certain your kids (and everyone else) will love. All I know is they've quickly become my family's favorites too.

treats

cowboy cookies

These cookies are always gone the day they're made. What I love most about this recipe is that it is easily adaptable: It's an "everything but the kitchen sink" type cookie, but you can add or omit any of the mix-ins. I think these are healthy enough to be called a breakfast cookie too.

MAKES 2 DOZEN

1 cup dairy-free margarine, softened

1 packed cup light brown sugar

1 cup granulated sugar

½ cup unsweetened applesauce

1 teaspoon vanilla extract

2¼ cups unbleached all-purpose flour or gluten-free flour blend

1 teaspoon baking soda

1 teaspoon baking powder

½ teaspoon salt

2 cups old-fashioned rolled oats

1 cup allergy-friendly chocolate chips

½ cup raisins, dried cranberries, or dried cherries (optional)

¼ cup unsweetened desiccated coconut (optional)

❋ Preheat the oven to 350°F and line two 13 x 18-inch rimmed baking sheets with parchment paper.

❋ In the bowl of an electric mixer fitted with the paddle attachment, combine the margarine, brown sugar, and granulated sugar and beat until the mixture is light and fluffy. Add the applesauce and vanilla and mix well.

❋ In a medium bowl, combine the flour, baking soda, baking powder, and salt, using a wire whisk. Add to the margarine mixture and thoroughly mix. Stir in the oats, chocolate chips, raisins, and coconut, if using, with a rubber spatula.

❄ Use a cookie scooper to scoop the dough, and drop balls, an inch apart, onto the prepared baking sheets. Bake for 15 to 17 minutes, until lightly browned around the edges. Cool completely on the baking sheets and store in an airtight container for up to 5 days.

banana oat cookies

This is yet another healthy lunch-box treat, filled with bananas and oats. My kids love it with chocolate chips, but raisins are a healthier and equally as delicious option.

MAKES 2 DOZEN

¾ cup dairy-free margarine, softened

1 cup sugar

1¼ cups mashed overripe bananas (about 3 bananas)

1¼ teaspoons vanilla extract

1¾ cups unbleached all-purpose flour or gluten-free flour blend

1 teaspoon salt

½ teaspoon baking soda

¾ teaspoon ground cinnamon

½ teaspoon ground nutmeg

1½ cups quick-cooking (not instant) or old-fashioned rolled oats

½ cup allergy-friendly chocolate chips, or raisins

❋ Preheat the oven to 400°F and line two 13 x 18-inch rimmed baking sheets with parchment paper.

❋ In the bowl of an electric mixer fitted with the paddle attachment, combine the margarine, sugar, mashed bananas, and vanilla and mix until smooth.

❋ In a medium bowl, combine the flour, salt, baking soda, cinnamon, and nutmeg using a wire whisk. Add to the margarine mixture and combine thoroughly. Stir in the oats and chocolate chips.

✳ Use a cookie scooper to scoop the dough into 1-inch balls, and drop them, an inch apart, onto the prepared baking sheets. Bake for 12 to 15 minutes, until lightly browned. Cool completely on the baking sheets. Store in an airtight container up to 3 days.

sugar and spice cookies

These cookies are among our favorites. They're the epitome of sugar and spice and everything nice. My kids love this cookie as a sweet after-school snack; it's also perfect for little lunch boxes.

MAKES 2 DOZEN

¾ cup dairy-free margarine, softened

½ cup sugar

½ packed cup light brown sugar

¼ cup unsweetened applesauce

¼ cup honey

2¾ cups unbleached all-purpose flour or gluten-free flour blend

2½ teaspoons baking soda

1 teaspoon ground cinnamon

1 teaspoon ground ginger

¼ teaspoon ground nutmeg

¼ teaspoon salt

SUGAR COATING

⅓ packed cup light brown sugar

¼ cup sugar

1 teaspoon ground cinnamon

✺ Preheat the oven to 350°F and line 2 rimmed baking sheets with parchment paper.

✺ In the bowl of an electric mixer fitted with the paddle attachment, combine the margarine, granulated sugar, and brown sugar and mix until light and fluffy. Add the applesauce and honey and mix well.

✳ In a medium bowl, combine the flour, baking soda, cinnamon, ginger, nutmeg, and salt, using a wire whisk. Add to the margarine mixture and mix well.

✳ **TO MAKE THE SUGAR COATING,** in a small bowl, combine the brown sugar, granulated sugar, and ground cinnamon.

✳ Roll the cookie dough into 1-inch balls. Roll the dough balls in the brown sugar mixture and place 1 inch apart on parchment paper. Bake for 12 to 15 minutes, until the cookies are lightly browned on top. Cool completely on the baking sheets and store in an airtight container up to 2 days.

cinnamon sour cream cookies

This type of cookie was popular during my grandparents' era. It's a classic cookie that deserves to be brought out of retirement and back into everyday treat rotation.

MAKES 2 DOZEN

1 cup dairy-free margarine, softened

1½ cups sugar

½ cup unsweetened applesauce

1¼ teaspoons vanilla extract

1 cup dairy-free sour cream

3½ cups unbleached all-purpose flour or gluten-free flour blend

1 teaspoon baking powder

½ teaspoon baking soda

½ teaspoon salt

CINNAMON-SUGAR TOPPING

½ cup sugar

1 teaspoon ground cinnamon

❋ Preheat the oven to 375°F and line 2 rimmed baking sheets with parchment paper.

❋ In the bowl of an electric mixer fitted with the paddle attachment, combine the margarine, sugar, applesauce, and vanilla and mix until light and fluffy. Slowly add the sour cream and mix until smooth.

❋ In a medium bowl, combine the flour, baking powder, baking soda, and salt using a wire whisk. Gradually add the flour mixture to the margarine mixture and mix until combined. Cover and refrigerate for at least 1 hour, and up to 8 hours.

✳ Remove the dough from the refrigerator and use a mini cookie scooper to scoop it, 1 inch apart, onto the baking sheets.

✳ **TO MAKE THE TOPPING,** combine the sugar and cinnamon and sprinkle generously over the tops of the cookies. Bake for 12 to 15 minutes, until puffy and lightly browned. Cool completely on the baking sheets and store up to 2 days in an airtight storage container.

chocolate sugar cookies

I love sugar cookies. My kids love chocolate sugar cookies even more. Of course, my kids love anything chocolate. This cookie is a chocolaty variation on my original sugar cookie recipe in my first book, The Food Allergy Mama's Baking Book. *We especially love to make it around Valentine's Day.*

MAKES 2 DOZEN

1 cup dairy-free margarine, softened

1½ cups sugar

½ cup unsweetened applesauce

2¼ teaspoons vanilla extract

3 cups unbleached all-purpose flour or gluten-free flour blend

¾ cup unsweetened cocoa powder

1 teaspoon baking soda

¼ teaspoon salt

Allergy-friendly colored sprinkles for topping (optional)

❊ Preheat the oven to 350°F and line 2 rimmed baking sheets with parchment paper.

❊ In the bowl of an electric mixer fitted with the paddle attachment, combine the margarine and sugar and mix until light and fluffy. Add the applesauce and vanilla and mix well.

❊ In a medium bowl, combine the flour, cocoa powder, baking soda, and salt using a wire whisk. Add the dry mixture to the wet mixture and mix until well incorporated. Cover and refrigerate the dough for at least 1 hour in the fridge or up to 8 hours. Alternatively, do a quick chill in the freezer for 30 minutes.

✳ Roll the dough out onto a lightly floured surface. Set out a small bowl of flour, dip a cookie cutter into the flour, and cut the dough into desired shapes. Top with sprinkles if you like, and bake for 10 to 13 minutes, until set. Cool completely on the baking sheets and store up to 2 days.

chocolate crinkles

I don't know one person who doesn't absolutely love these cookies. I've made them countless times for holidays, birthdays, teacher gifts, and even just as an after-school snack. They stay fresh for a few days, making them the perfect treat to make ahead of time.

MAKES 2 DOZEN

½ cup vegetable or canola oil

1¾ cups granulated sugar

1 cup unsweetened applesauce

1 cup unsweetened cocoa powder

2¼ teaspoons vanilla extract

2¼ cups unbleached all-purpose flour or gluten-free flour blend

2 teaspoons baking powder

¼ teaspoon salt

1 cup confectioners' sugar, plus more as needed

❋ In the bowl of an electric mixer fitted with the paddle attachment, combine the oil, granulated sugar, applesauce, cocoa powder, and vanilla and mix until well combined.

❋ In a medium bowl, combine the flour, baking powder, and salt using a wire whisk. Add the dry ingredients to the wet ingredients and mix until combined. Put the dough into a resealable plastic bag or a small bowl covered with plastic wrap and freeze until well chilled, about 1 hour. It will be sticky. (Alternatively, chill in the refrigerator for 3 to 4 hours or overnight.)

❋ Preheat the oven to 350°F and line 2 rimmed baking sheets with parchment paper.

✳ Place the confectioners' sugar in a small bowl. Lightly flour your hands with additional confectioners' sugar, scoop out 1-inch balls of dough, and roll them into perfect balls. Drop into the bowl of confectioners' sugar and roll until completely covered with sugar. Place 2 inches apart on the prepared baking sheets and bake for about 10 minutes, until the cookies are just set. Do not overbake. Cool completely on the baking sheets. These may be stored up to 3 days in an airtight container.

chocolate thumbprint cookies

Every time I make these little gems, they are gone the day I make them. My kids and their friends tell me it's one of their favorites, and they have been known to grab four or five cookies at a time! I love them whether filled with melted chocolate or red raspberry preserves.

MAKES 2 DOZEN

1 cup dairy-free margarine, softened

1⅓ cups sugar

¼ cup unsweetened applesauce

1½ tablespoons vanilla extract

2¼ cups unbleached all-purpose flour or gluten-free flour blend

⅔ cup unsweetened cocoa powder

½ teaspoon salt

1 cup allergy-friendly chocolate chips or 1 cup red raspberry preserves for filling

❉ Preheat the oven to 350°F and line 2 baking sheets with parchment paper.

❉ In the bowl of an electric mixer fitted with the paddle attachment, combine the margarine and 1 cup of the sugar and beat until light and fluffy. Add the applesauce and vanilla and mix well.

❉ In a medium bowl, combine the flour, cocoa powder, and salt using a wire whisk. Add to the margarine mixture and mix until combined.

❉ Roll the cookie dough into 1-inch balls and roll in the remaining ⅓ cup sugar. Place on the prepared baking sheets, about 1 inch apart, and bake for 5 minutes. Use the back of a melon ball scooper or your thumb to make an indentation in the middle of each cookie. Return the cookies to the oven and bake for 4 to 5 additional minutes, until the cookies are just set. Do not overbake. Cool completely on the baking sheets.

❋ Make the filling. If using chocolate chips, place them in a microwave-safe bowl and microwave in 20-second increments until the chocolate chips are beginning to melt. Use a rubber spatula to stir the rest of the chocolate chips until they are melted. Use a ½-teaspoon measuring spoon to fill the center of each cookie with the melted chocolate. Alternatively, fill the centers with ½ teaspoon of raspberry preserves. Store up to two days in an airtight container.

soy butter sandwich cookies (aka faux girl scout do-si-dos)

I've been in love with Girl Scout Cookies my whole life. So every year when a Girl Scout inevitably comes knocking on my door, it pains me that I can't buy one of my all-time favorites, Peanut Butter Sandwich Cookies, aka Do-Si-Dos. Finally, I decided I had to re-create this amazing little treat. My kids absolutely adore these cookies. They are as great as, if not better than, the legendary Do-Si-Dos.

MAKES ABOUT 1 DOZEN

½ cup dairy-free margarine, softened

½ cup granulated sugar

½ packed cup light brown sugar

½ cup creamy soy or sunflower butter

¼ cup unsweetened applesauce

1 teaspoon vanilla extract

¾ cup unbleached all-purpose flour or gluten-free flour blend

½ teaspoon baking powder

½ teaspoon baking soda

⅛ teaspoon salt

1½ cups old-fashioned rolled oats

SOY BUTTER FILLING

1 cup dairy-free margarine, softened

1½ cups creamy soy or sunflower butter

½ teaspoon vanilla extract

½ cup confectioners' sugar

❋ Preheat the oven to 350°F and line 2 rimmed baking sheets with parchment paper.

❋ In the bowl of an electric mixer fitted with the paddle attachment, combine the margarine, granulated sugar, brown sugar, soy butter, applesauce, and vanilla and mix until creamy.

❋ In a medium bowl, combine the flour, baking powder, baking soda, and salt using a wire whisk. Add the flour mixture to the soy butter mixture and combine well. Add the oats and stir well using a rubber spatula.

❋ Use a small cookie scooper to scoop the dough 1 inch apart onto the prepared baking sheets. Bake for 10 to 12 minutes, until lightly browned. Cool completely on the baking sheets.

❋ **TO MAKE THE FILLING,** combine the margarine, soy butter, and vanilla in the bowl of an electric mixer fitted with the paddle attachment. Add the confectioners' sugar and stir until combined.

❋ To fill the cookies, use a butter knife to spread the soy butter filling between 2 soy butter cookies. To store, wrap each cookie individually in plastic wrap. The cookies will keep for up to 2 days.

oatmeal crème pies

Readers of my blog, www.foodallergymama.com, already know that I have quite a sweet tooth and an obsession with Little Debbie Snacks. I grew up loving all her treats, but my favorite was the Oatmeal Crème Pies. They were individually wrapped in all their glory, perfect for my lunch box. I rediscovered that love when I was pregnant with my third child, Matthew, and those pies were the only thing that cured my terrible morning sickness. I went through a box every two days. I wanted to re-create the magic of these pies for my son John, and all my other kids, who never get to have any Little Debbie treats in our house. It is one of my all-time favorite recipes, and I promise it will be one of yours too.

MAKES 24

COOKIES

¾ cup dairy-free margarine, softened

1¾ packed cups light brown sugar

½ cup unsweetened applesauce

1 teaspoon vanilla extract

2 tablespoons water

2¼ cups unbleached all-purpose flour or gluten-free flour blend

1 teaspoon ground cinnamon

⅛ teaspoon ground nutmeg

1 teaspoon baking powder

2 teaspoons baking soda

½ teaspoon salt

2 cups quick-cooking oats (not instant)

CRÈME FILLING

4 cups confectioners' sugar

2 teaspoons cream of tartar

2½ teaspoons vanilla extract

5 tablespoons soy or rice milk

½ cup dairy-free shortening

❋ Preheat the oven to 425°F and line 3 rimmed baking sheets with parchment paper.

❋ **MAKE THE COOKIES:** In the bowl of an electric mixer fitted with the paddle attachment, combine the margarine, brown sugar, applesauce, vanilla, and water and mix until combined well.

❋ In a medium bowl, combine the flour, cinnamon, nutmeg, baking powder, baking soda, and salt using a wire whisk. Add to the margarine mixture and mix well. Stir in the oats using a rubber spatula.

❋ Use a mini cookie scooper to scoop the dough 1 inch apart onto the prepared baking sheets. Bake for 7 to 10 minutes, until golden brown. Let cool completely on the baking sheets.

❋ **WHILE THE COOKIES ARE BAKING, MAKE THE FILLING:** Combine all the filling ingredients in the bowl of an electric mixer fitted with the paddle attachment and mix until creamy.

❋ When the cookies are cooled, spread a generous amount (I love the crème part to seep through the edges for the ultimate flavor) on the flat side of one cookie, then top with another cookie, flat side down. Wrap each "pie" in plastic wrap; they will keep for up to 2 days.

whoopie pies

Whoopie pies have made quite a comeback in recent years. Everyone loves a great sandwich cookie that resembles a cake. This is a great recipe to make with your kids; have them do all the frosting and assembling!

MAKES 24

1 cup dairy-free margarine, softened

2 cups sugar

½ cup unsweetened applesauce

2½ teaspoons vanilla extract

4¼ cups unbleached all-purpose flour or gluten-free flour blend

2 teaspoons baking soda

¼ teaspoon salt

1 cup unsweetened cocoa powder

1 cup dairy-free sour cream

1 cup hot water

FILLING

¾ cup dairy-free margarine, softened

2¾ cups confectioners' sugar

4 teaspoons vanilla extract

2 teaspoons soy or rice milk

❋ Preheat the oven to 350°F and line 3 rimmed baking sheets with parchment paper.

❋ In the bowl of an electric mixer fitted with the paddle attachment, cream the margarine until smooth. Add the sugar and beat until light and fluffy. Add the applesauce and vanilla and mix thoroughly.

✳ In a medium bowl, combine the flour, baking soda, salt, and cocoa powder, using a wire whisk. Add the flour mixture in thirds, alternating with the sour cream and the water, to the margarine mixture.

✳ Use a cookie scooper to drop tablespoonfuls of batter onto the prepared baking sheets. Bake one sheet at a time for 10 to 12 minutes, until a cookie bounces back slightly when touched in the center. Lightly flatten each cookie with the palm of your hand if you like a slightly less puffy cookie. Cool completely on the baking sheets.

✳ **WHILE THE COOKIES ARE COOLING, PREPARE THE FILLING:** In the bowl of an electric mixer fitted with the paddle attachment, cream the margarine until smooth. Add the confectioners' sugar, about 1 cup at a time, until the mixture is light and fluffy. Add the vanilla and soy milk and mix on medium-high speed for about 2 minutes, until it resembles a creamy frosting. If you'd like your frosting a little firmer, put it in the fridge for a few minutes.

✳ When the cookies have cooled, use a small butter knife to spread a thin layer of frosting on the flat side of one cookie, and top with another cookie to make a whoopie pie. Continue with the remaining cookies and filling. Wrap each one individually in plastic wrap and store up to 2 days.

chocolate chip oat bars

These delicious little bars are easy to make, bake, and take. I love to make them for an after-school treat. You could add ½ cup dried cranberries to make the bars taste like granola bars.

MAKES 16

⅓ cup dairy-free shortening

⅔ packed cup light brown sugar

¼ cup unsweetened applesauce

1 teaspoon vanilla extract

1 cup unbleached all-purpose flour or gluten-free flour blend

¼ teaspoon baking soda

¼ teaspoon salt

1¼ cups quick-cooking oats (not instant)

1 cup allergy-friendly chocolate chips

❊ Preheat the oven to 350°F. Line a 9-inch square Pyrex baking pan with foil and coat with dairy-free cooking spray.

❊ In the bowl of an electric mixer fitted with the paddle attachment, combine the shortening, brown sugar, applesauce, and vanilla and mix until smooth.

❊ In a medium bowl, combine the flour, baking soda, and salt using a wire whisk and add to the shortening mixture. Stir in the oats and chocolate chips.

❊ Spread the mixture into the prepared baking dish and bake for 30 minutes, or until lightly browned on top. Cool completely and cut into bars.

spiced applesauce bars

This is yet another easy and fast treat to make with ingredients you probably already have on hand. It smells incredible baking in the oven and is perfect year-round.

MAKES 36 BARS

½ cup dairy-free margarine, softened

1 cup granulated sugar

1¾ cups unsweetened applesauce

1¼ teaspoons vanilla extract

2 cups unbleached all-purpose flour or gluten-free flour blend

2 teaspoons baking soda

1 teaspoon ground cinnamon

¼ teaspoon ground cloves

¼ teaspoon ground nutmeg

¼ teaspoon salt

¾ cup raisins (optional)

Confectioners' sugar for sprinkling

✻ Preheat the oven to 350°F and coat a baking pan or sheet (see Note) with dairy-free cooking spray.

✻ In the bowl of an electric mixer fitted with the paddle attachment, combine the margarine with the granulated sugar and mix until light and fluffy. Add ¼ cup of the applesauce and the vanilla and beat well.

✻ In a medium bowl, combine the flour, baking soda, cinnamon, cloves, nutmeg, and salt using a wire whisk. Add to the margarine mixture and stir until just combined. Stir in the remaining 1½ cups applesauce and the raisins, if using. Spread the batter into the prepared pan.

✽ Bake for 25 to 30 minutes, if using a 9 x 13-inch pan, or 22 to 25 minutes, if using a 10 x 15-inch sheet, until lightly browned and an inserted cake tester or toothpick comes out clean. Cool completely, cut into squares, and sprinkle with confectioners' sugar before serving.

NOTE • Use either a 9 x 13-inch baking pan or a 10 x 15-inch rimmed baking sheet, depending on how thick you'd like your bars.

apple cinnamon crunch bars

This treat is a cross between a warm apple crisp and a warm apple pie. I love the crunchy topping.

MAKES 12 BARS

CRUST

2 cups unbleached all-purpose flour or gluten-free flour blend

½ cup sugar

1½ cups quick-cooking oats (not instant)

½ teaspoon baking powder

¼ teaspoon salt

1 cup dairy-free margarine, cut into small cubes

2 tablespoons water

APPLE FILLING

4 cups peeled and thinly sliced apples (use any variety you have on hand; I like to use a mixture of varieties, such as Braeburn, Cortland, Gala, and Granny Smith)

¼ cup unbleached all-purpose flour or gluten-free flour blend

¾ packed cup light brown sugar

1 teaspoon ground cinnamon

¼ teaspoon ground nutmeg

1 teaspoon vanilla extract

❋ Preheat the oven to 350°F and coat a 9 x 13-inch glass baking dish with dairy-free cooking spray.

❋ **TO MAKE THE CRUST,** in a medium bowl, combine the flour, sugar, ½ cup of the oats, the baking powder, and salt using a wire whisk. Add the cubes of margarine and cut them in with a pastry cutter or 2 knives. Once the mixture is the size of peas (some bigger chunks are fine too), add the water and stir with a rubber spatula until incorporated.

❀ Press half of the mixture into the prepared baking dish, using the back of a measuring cup or spoon, or use your hands (slightly wet them first).

❀ Add the remaining 1 cup oats to the remaining flour mixture in the bowl and mix thoroughly, using the rubber spatula.

❀ **TO MAKE THE FILLING,** in a medium bowl, combine the apples, flour, brown sugar, cinnamon, nutmeg, and vanilla. Pour the apple mixture over the crust mixture in the baking dish. Sprinkle the remaining flour-oat mixture over the apples and bake for 45 minutes, or until the top is lightly golden brown. Cool completely and cut into squares.

oatmeal fudge bars

This recipe signifies everything I love about baking: It's easy and fast, and it tastes rich and decadent. I promise no one will ever miss the dairy or eggs.

MAKES 16

OAT LAYER

½ cup dairy-free shortening

1 packed cup light brown sugar

¼ cup unsweetened applesauce

1 teaspoon vanilla extract

1 cup unbleached all-purpose flour or gluten-free flour blend

½ teaspoon baking soda

½ teaspoon salt

2 cups old-fashioned rolled oats or quick-cooking oats (not instant)

FUDGE LAYER

1½ cups allergy-friendly chocolate chips

¼ cup dairy-free margarine

1 tablespoon water

½ cup unbleached all-purpose flour or gluten-free flour

¼ cup sugar

❋ Preheat the oven to 350°F and coat an 8-inch square Pyrex baking dish with dairy-free cooking spray.

❋ In the bowl of an electric mixer fitted with the paddle attachment (or use a medium bowl with a wooden spoon), combine the shortening and brown sugar and mix until light and fluffy. Add the applesauce and vanilla and thoroughly combine.

✳ In a small bowl, combine the flour, baking soda, and salt, using a wire whisk. Add to the shortening mixture and stir well. Stir in the oats. Reserve 1 cup of the oat mixture for the topping. Spread the rest into the prepared baking dish using the back of a spoon or your fingers (wet them first). Set aside.

✳ **MAKE THE FUDGE LAYER:** In a microwave-safe bowl, combine the chocolate chips and margarine. Heat in the microwave for 20 seconds at a time, until the chips are just melted. Add the water and stir with a rubber spatula until combined. In a small bowl, combine the flour and sugar using a wire whisk. Add the chocolate mixture to the flour mixture and stir until combined.

✳ Spread the fudge layer over the oat layer. Sprinkle the top with the reserved oat mixture and spread with the back of a spoon or your fingers (wet them first). Bake for 20 to 25 minutes, until lightly browned. Cool completely before cutting into squares.

chocolate pudding cups

Pudding is a classic kids' dessert, yet nearly every single recipe or packaged brand contains eggs and/or milk. My son John really wanted to try real chocolate pudding after seeing kids in his lunchroom devour it. This version takes about ten minutes to make, and is so much healthier than those store-bought versions. To make the chocolate shaving garnish, use a vegetable peeler to shave a dairy, egg, and nut free chocolate bar.

SERVES 6

⅓ cup sugar

⅓ cup unsweetened cocoa powder

¼ teaspoon salt

3 tablespoons cornstarch mixed with 2 tablespoons cold water

2 cups soy or rice milk

1 cup silken tofu

1 teaspoon vanilla extract

2 tablespoons cornstarch mixed with 2 tablespoons cold water

1 cup allergy-friendly chocolate chips

1 tablespoon dairy-free margarine

½ cup chocolate shavings

❋ In a medium saucepan, combine the sugar, cocoa powder, and salt, using a wire whisk. Add the 3 tablespoons cornstarch mixture and stir with a whisk.

❋ In a blender, combine the soy milk, tofu, and vanilla and blend until smooth. Add to the cocoa mixture and cook over medium-low heat for 5 to 8 minutes, until combined, stirring constantly with a wire whisk. Add the 2 tablespoons cornstarch mixture and cook for an additional 2 to 3 minutes, until the mixture is thickened and creamy. Turn off the heat and stir in the chocolate chips and margarine with a rubber spatula until melted.

❋ Divide the pudding mixture evenly among six 6-ounce ramekins or 1 large glass bowl. Cover the pudding with plastic wrap, touching the surface of the pudding directly to prevent a skin from forming (if you like pudding skin, don't let the plastic wrap touch the pudding).

❋ Place in the refrigerator to chill for at least 2 hours or up to 1 day. Serve with the chocolate shavings on top.

chocolate pudding cake

I love to serve this cake for dinner guests or for my husband on Valentine's Day. It is warm and gooey and incredibly easy to whip up. Assemble all the ingredients and put it into the oven while your guests arrive. Your house will smell divine and the cake will be ready when you are ready to serve it.

SERVES 6

½ cup soy or rice milk

¼ cup vegetable or canola oil

1¼ teaspoons vanilla extract

1 cup unbleached all-purpose flour or gluten-free flour blend

1⅓ cups sugar

½ cup unsweetened cocoa powder

2 teaspoons baking powder

¼ teaspoon baking soda

¼ teaspoon salt

¾ cup allergy-friendly chocolate chips

1 cup boiling water

❋ Preheat the oven to 350°F and coat an 8-inch square glass baking dish with dairy-free cooking spray.

❋ In a medium bowl, combine the soy milk, oil, and vanilla using a wire whisk.

❋ In a separate medium bowl, combine the flour, ⅔ cup of the sugar, ¼ cup of the cocoa powder, the baking powder, baking soda, and salt using a wire whisk. Add the soy milk mixture to the flour mixture and stir with a rubber spatula until thoroughly mixed. Stir in the chocolate chips.

✳ Spread the batter into the prepared baking dish.

✳ In a small bowl, combine the remaining ²/₃ cup sugar and ¼ cup cocoa powder. Sprinkle evenly over the top of the batter and pour 1 cup boiling water over the top. Do not stir.

✳ Bake for 30 to 35 minutes, until the cake is just set in the center and a cake tester or toothpick inserted in the middle comes out with just a few crumbs. Remove from the oven and serve warm or at room temperature. The cake can be scooped out with a large spoon while still warm, and then cooled and cut into slices.

fudge brownie pie

I've loved Bakers Square, a popular midwestern pie chain restaurant, ever since it was originally called Poppin Fresh. Which, I guess, is a long time ago. I've been a pie girl my entire life. And I love that my daughter, Chloe, loves pie as much as I do, and accompanies me to Bakers Square on Wednesday for Free Pie. I didn't want to leave out my boys at home, especially John, so I created this knockoff of the Hot Fudge Brownie à la Mode served at the restaurant. It's delicious served warm, with a side of allergy-friendly ice cream.

SERVES 6

½ cup dairy-free margarine, softened

¾ cup sugar

½ cup silken tofu

1¼ teaspoons vanilla extract

⅔ cup unbleached all-purpose flour or gluten-free flour blend

½ cup unsweetened cocoa powder

½ teaspoon baking powder

½ teaspoon salt

⅔ cup plus ½ cup allergy-friendly chocolate chips

Dairy-free, allergy-friendly ice cream for serving

❋ Preheat the oven to 350°F and coat a 9-inch Pyrex pie plate with dairy-free cooking spray.

❋ In the bowl of an electric mixer fitted with the paddle attachment, combine the margarine and sugar and mix until light and fluffy. Add the tofu and vanilla and mix well.

✺ In a medium bowl, combine the flour, cocoa, baking powder, and salt, using a wire whisk. Add to the margarine mixture and combine well. Stir in ²/₃ cup of the chocolate chips using a rubber spatula and transfer the batter to the prepared pie plate.

✺ Bake for 25 minutes, or until an inserted cake tester or toothpick comes out just clean (a few crumbs attached to the toothpick will ensure a moist pie).

✺ **MEANWHILE, MAKE A CHOCOLATE DRIZZLE** by melting the remaining ½ cup chocolate chips: Place them in a microwave-safe bowl and microwave for 30 seconds to 1 minute, until melted.

✺ Cool slightly before slicing, or cool completely, slice, and reheat the slices in the microwave when ready to serve. Serve each slice with a small rounded scoop of ice cream and a generous drizzle of chocolate sauce.

favorite chocolate sheet cake with chocolate ganache

I often call this cake my after-school cake, because it's my children's ultimate treat after a long day at school. It's the perfect cake to make for gatherings, holidays, and birthdays too. I love to make it for my own birthday because it is so darn easy. The cake will keep, covered, for up to 3 days in the refrigerator; heat individual slices for 10 seconds in the microwave to slightly soften the ganache before serving.

SERVES 8

3¼ cups unbleached all-purpose flour or gluten-free flour blend

1¾ cups sugar

¾ cup unsweetened cocoa powder

2¼ teaspoons baking powder

2 teaspoons baking soda

¾ teaspoon salt

⅔ cup dairy-free margarine, melted

1¾ cups dairy-free buttermilk (see page 6)

2¼ teaspoons vanilla extract

CHOCOLATE GANACHE

2 cups allergy-friendly chocolate chips

½ cup soy or rice milk

½ teaspoon vanilla extract

✳ **TO MAKE THE CAKE,** preheat the oven to 350°F and coat a 9 x 13-inch baking dish with dairy-free cooking spray.

✳ In a large bowl, combine the flour, sugar, cocoa powder, baking powder, baking soda, and salt using a wire whisk.

✳ In the bowl of an electric mixer fitted with the paddle attachment, combine the melted margarine, buttermilk, and vanilla. Add the flour mixture and mix well. Pour the batter into the prepared baking dish and bake for 35 to 40 minutes, until a cake tester or toothpick comes out clean. Cool completely in the pan.

✳ **MEANWHILE, MAKE THE CHOCOLATE GANACHE:** Place the chocolate chips, soy milk, and vanilla in a small saucepan over very low heat and heat, stirring with a rubber spatula, until most of the chocolate chips are melted. Remove from the heat and stir with the spatula until the remaining chocolate chips are melted.

✳ Once the cake is cooled, pour the ganache over the cake and spread it out evenly. Store the cake covered in the refrigerator.

chocolate banana cupcakes with chocolate frosting

This cupcake is one of the best I've ever tasted. It's also one of the simplest I've ever made.

MAKES 12

CUPCAKES

1 cup mashed banana

½ cup room-temperature water

¼ cup dairy-free buttermilk (see page 6)

¼ cup vegetable or canola oil

1 teaspoon vanilla extract

1 cup unbleached all-purpose flour or gluten-free flour blend

¾ cup sugar

⅓ cup unsweetened cocoa powder

1 teaspoon baking soda

1 teaspoon baking powder

½ teaspoon salt

⅓ cup allergy-friendly chocolate chips

CHOCOLATE FROSTING

½ cup dairy-free margarine, softened

¼ cup unsweetened cocoa powder

2 tablespoons soy or rice milk

½ teaspoon vanilla extract

2 cups confectioners' sugar

❋ Preheat the oven to 350ºF and line a 12-cup muffin pan with paper liners.

✳ **TO MAKE THE CUPCAKES,** in a medium bowl, combine the mashed banana, water, buttermilk, oil, and vanilla.

✳ In a medium bowl, combine the flour, sugar, cocoa powder, baking soda, baking powder, and salt using a wire whisk. Add the liquid ingredients to the dry ingredients and stir until combined. Stir in the chocolate chips.

✳ Divide the batter evenly among the paper cups. Bake for 20 to 25 minutes, until a cake tester or toothpick comes out clean. Remove from the oven and cool completely in the pan.

✳ **TO MAKE THE FROSTING,** combine the margarine, cocoa powder, soy milk, and vanilla in the bowl of an electric mixer fitted with the paddle attachment. Add the confectioners' sugar, a little at a time, and mix until combined. Turn the mixer to medium-high and mix for 3 to 4 minutes, until creamy. Frost the cooled cupcakes.

pumpkin cupcakes with dairy-free cream cheese frosting

These are excellent cupcakes to serve around the holidays when pumpkin—canned or fresh—is abundant. Kids love them!

MAKES 12

CUPCAKES

½ cup dairy-free margarine, softened

¾ cup sugar

2 tablespoons water

1¼ teaspoons vanilla extract

1 cup pumpkin puree (canned or fresh)

1½ cups unbleached all-purpose flour or gluten-free flour blend

1 teaspoon baking soda

1¼ teaspoons ground cinnamon

¼ teaspoon ground nutmeg

¼ teaspoon ground ginger

¼ teaspoon salt

FROSTING

½ cup dairy-free cream cheese, softened

1 tablespoon soy or rice milk

¼ cup dairy-free margarine, softened

½ teaspoon vanilla extract

3 cups confectioners' sugar

❊ Preheat the oven to 350°F and line 12 muffin cups or 24 mini muffin cups with paper liners.

✻ In the bowl of an electric mixer fitted with the paddle attachment, combine the margarine and sugar and mix until light and fluffy. Add the water, vanilla, and pumpkin puree and thoroughly combine.

✻ In a medium bowl, combine the flour, baking soda, cinnamon, nutmeg, ginger, and salt using a wire whisk. Add to the pumpkin mixture and combine thoroughly.

✻ Divide the batter evenly among the muffin cups. Bake for 18 to 20 minutes, until an inserted cake tester or toothpick comes out clean. Cool completely in the pan.

✻ **TO MAKE THE FROSTING,** combine the cream cheese, soy milk, margarine, and vanilla in the bowl of an electric mixer fitted with the paddle attachment and mix until smooth. Add the confectioners' sugar, a little at a time, and mix well. Cover and refrigerate for 30 minutes before using.

✻ When the cupcakes are cooled and the frosting is chilled, either dip the cupcakes into the frosting or use a small butter knife to frost them. Keep refrigerated until ready to serve.

red velvet double chocolate chip cupcakes

This is a fantastic and gorgeously red cupcake that is great for holidays and birthdays. People are always shocked when they learn they are made without any dairy or eggs.

MAKES 24

CUPCAKES

¾ cup dairy-free margarine, softened

1½ cups sugar

1 cup dairy-free buttermilk (see page 6)

½ cup silken tofu

1 tablespoon vinegar

1½ teaspoons vanilla extract

6 tablespoons liquid red food coloring

2¼ cups plus 1 tablespoon unbleached all-purpose flour or gluten-free flour blend

1½ teaspoons baking soda

3 tablespoons unsweetened cocoa powder

¼ teaspoon salt

1 cup allergy-friendly chocolate chips

FROSTING

½ cup dairy-free margarine, softened

¾ cup dairy-free cream cheese, softened

1¼ teaspoons vanilla extract

3½ cups confectioners' sugar

¼ cup unsweetened cocoa powder

❋ Preheat the oven to 350°F and line 24 muffin cups with paper liners.

✳ In the bowl of an electric mixer fitted with the paddle attachment, cream together the margarine and sugar until light and fluffy.

✳ In a large measuring cup or bowl, whisk together the buttermilk, tofu, vinegar, vanilla, and food coloring. Add to the margarine mixture and mix on low speed until thoroughly incorporated.

✳ In a medium bowl, combine 2¼ cups of the flour, the baking soda, cocoa powder, and salt using a wire whisk. Add to the margarine and buttermilk mixture and mix on low speed until just combined. Scrape down the sides and turn the speed up to medium-high. Beat for about 2 minutes, making sure the food coloring is evenly distributed throughout the batter.

✳ In a small bowl, mix the chocolate chips with the remaining 1 tablespoon flour and stir into the batter using a rubber spatula.

✳ Divide the batter among the paper cups and bake for 15 to 20 minutes, until an inserted cake tester or toothpick comes out clean. Cool completely in the pans.

✳ **TO MAKE THE FROSTING,** in the bowl of an electric mixer fitted with the paddle attachment, cream together the margarine, cream cheese, and vanilla. Slowly add the confectioners' sugar and cocoa powder and mix on low speed for 1 minute. Increase the speed to medium and beat for 4 to 6 minutes, until light and fluffy. Cover and chill before using.

✳ When the cupcakes are cooled and the frosting is chilled, either dip the cupcakes into the frosting or use a small butter knife to frost them. Keep refrigerated until ready to serve.

7

❉

Before I had a child with food allergies, I used to love to go out
to eat, and when I threw parties I always opted to cater or order
in cakes and desserts. However, after John's diagnosis, I never
imagined how wonderful and satisfying it could be to create all
these meals for parties, family get-togethers, and even simple
family meals. Here are just a few ways to mix up the recipes in
this book to make a delicious yet fast and easy family meal.
Happy cooking and baking!

BIRTHDAY BREAKFAST

Every time one of my children celebrates a birthday, I always bring him or her a special breakfast in bed served on a sunny yellow tray, with fresh flowers, and a special "Happy Birthday" plate that only comes out for the special occasion. My kids absolutely love it and look forward to a day of extra-special attention. I serve their favorite breakfast, which usually involves some sort of chocolate!

Powerhouse Smoothie (page 33)
Classic French Toast (page 39)
Double Chocolate Chip Muffins (page 52)
Mixed fresh fruit

PERFECT SCHOOL DAY BREAKFAST

I often find that it is a lot easier to serve one hot breakfast to five hungry kids (including four hungry boys!) than to ask who wants which cereal. Most mornings I make pancakes or waffles, and make extra because they freeze really well.

Tropical Smoothie (page 32)
Cinnamon Spice Pancakes (page 41)
Mixed fresh fruit

FAVORITE LUNCH-BOX MEAL

We generally make most of our lunches at home, so it can get monotonous if I don't change it up and serve something different from the usual turkey or soy butter sandwich. I love to serve thermoses of soups or containers of the previous night's supper. The pasta salad is my kids' favorite, hands down, and it's really easy to make the night before.

Broccoli and Chicken Pasta Salad (page 78)
Fresh fruit
Veggie sticks
Sugar and Spice Cookies (page 188)

WEEKEND LUNCH AT HOME

Weeks are often jam-packed with sports games and practices in our house, but we love to eat lunch together as a family as much as possible. If I have some extra time I will make soup and sandwiches. It's a great way to slow down, even if for just thirty minutes.

Creamy Tomato Soup (page 101)
Turkey and Dairy-Free Cheese Panini (page 83)
Citrus Salad with Jicama (page 74)
Soy Butter Sandwich Cookies (page 198)

BIRTHDAY PIZZA PARTY

Ah, the birthday party. Moms of food allergic kids can pretty much count on making and baking for the party, but this is actually a good thing! Kids would much prefer a homemade cake, and make-your-own pizzas rather than the greasy pizza served at traditional parties. I know my non-food-allergic kids don't even like the neon-tinted grocery store cupcakes. Invite a few kids over to play ball and cook—they'll have a blast!

Party Mix (page 15)
Rocky Road Popcorn (page 19)
Fresh cut veggies and baked chips with Dill Dip (page 21)
Make-Your-Own Pizza Bar (page 158)
Favorite Chocolate Sheet Cake with Chocolate Ganache (page 217)

HOLIDAY MORNING BRUNCH

Everyone wants an easy, special, but mostly make-ahead breakfast or brunch menu for holiday mornings. I love to make the strata and chocolate chip cinnamon rolls the night before, and then just put everything in the oven the next morning.

Vegetable Strata (page 36)
Chocolate Chip Cinnamon Rolls (page 66)
Fresh fruit salad

EASY WEEKNIGHT SUPPER

Making supper during the week can be tricky, especially when you're juggling kids, homework, and carpools. I love this menu because it's very easy to make a double batch of the sloppy joes and freeze the rest for another night.

Turkey Sloppy Joes (page 144)
Roasted Sweet Potato Wedges (page 171)
Chocolate Chip Oat Bars (page 204)

SUNDAY SUPPER

It used to be that Sunday was a day of rest and relaxation. A beautiful roast would cook in the oven all day, to be shared by the family for an early dinner. I love the idea of slowing down as much as possible on Sunday, especially before the start of a busy week. It's also a great strategy, because you can stretch the leftovers into another fast-and-easy meal later in the week.

Weeknight Double Roast Chicken (page 139)
Roasted Root Vegetables (page 172)
Baked Cornbread (page 179)
Chocolate Pudding Cake (page 213)

SOUP FOR SUPPER

It's great to make a nice hearty soup for dinner that's warm and so good for you.

Tomato, Chicken, and Gnocchi Soup (page 108)
Spinach Salad with Champagne Vinaigrette (page 75)
Chocolate Thumbprint Cookies (page 196)

SLEEPOVER SUPPER

When kids have their friends over for a sleepover, they want fun, kid-friendly food that actually tastes good. Fast food just doesn't cut it. I love to serve classic kid-friendly meals, but fresher and healthier.

Cinnamon-Sugar Popcorn (page 18)
Chicken Tenders (page 131)
Mini Corndogs (page 92)
Fresh cut vegetables and baked chips with French Onion Dip (page 20)
Oatmeal Crème Pies (page 200)

SICK-DAY SUPPER

We've all had to endure long days and nights of helping our kids through being sick. I've found that sometimes the best medicine is the simplest: love. Kids just want you there next to them when they're unwell, and if you can serve them a warm soup, even better.

Oma's Warm Milk (page 29)
Cinnamon Toast (page 30)
Easy Chicken Pasta Soup (page 96)

COMPANY-IS-COMING-OVER SUPPER

As much as we all love a good dinner out, many of us yearn and crave classic family food. When I have family and friends coming over for dinner, I love to serve something easy and not at all fussy.

Grandma Rudnicki's Bolognese Sauce (page 124)
Egg-free pasta or Potato Gnocchi (page 126)
Roasted Cauliflower (page 173)
Garlic Bread (page 26)
Fudge Brownie Pie (page 215)

Food Allergy Awareness Resources

Allergy Apparel

My favorite site for cool EpiPen holders, belts, baking accessories, lunch boxes, and allergy-aware tees.

www.allergyapparel.com

Allergy Kids Foundation

Another fantastic resource for parents with food-allergic kids.

www.allergykids.com

Allergy Moms

http://www.allergymoms.com

Creator Gina Clowes is a food allergy powerhouse—a food allergy coach, speaker, author, and advocate. Her advocacy efforts are among the most recognized by food allergy parents everywhere. If you need help getting your school to comply with 504 accommodations, Gina is the food allergy mama to call first.

American Academy of Allergy, Asthma & Immunology

555 East Wells Street

Milwaukee, WI 53202-3823

www.aaaai.org

Best Allergy Sites

A one-stop shop of the best allergy resources and blogs.

www.bestallergysites.com

The Food Allergy Experience

By Dr. Ruchi Gupta, MD, MPH, and Denise Bunning. A fantastic book filled with tips, guides, resources and helpful quotes from parents, doctors and teachers about how to navigate through the world of food allergy.

www.foodallergyexperience.com

FARE

A merger between The Food Allergy & Anaphylaxis Network (FAAN) and the Food Allergy Initiative (FAI), created in 2012 and dedicated to food allergy research and education.

7925 Jones Branch Drive

McLean, VA 22102

www.foodallergy.org

Kids with Food Allergies

One of my favorite sites for support and resources.

www.kidswithfoodallergies.org

MOCHA: Mothers of Children Having Allergies

www.mochallergies.org

info@mochallergies.org

MedicAlert Jewelry/MedicAlert Foundation

2323 Colorado Avenue

Turlock, CA 95382

www.medicalert.org

The Nut-Free Mom

Aka Jenny Kales. She's a great advocate for food allergy mamas everywhere, and writes for our favorite allergy-aware magazine, *Allergic Living.* I check her site regularly for the latest in food allergy news.

www.nut-freemom.blogspot.com

Allergic Living

This is a must-read magazine for tips, recipes, and newsworthy articles.

http://allergicliving.com

Divvies

Lori Sandler's site for the best mail-order dairy, egg, and nut free treats.

www.divvies.com

Cybele Pascal, the Allergy-Friendly Cook

Cybele's site is one of my favorites for completely allergen-free recipes. Her site is a must visit for moms of kids with food allergies.

www.cybelepascal.com

Kim & Scott's Gourmet Pretzels

I've known and loved Kim and Scott for years and admire their dedication to producing the best allergy-aware nut-free soft pretzels. They offer a gluten-free version as well. Their pretzels are available in most grocery store freezer sections.
www.kimandscotts.com

Illinois State Board of Education Food Allergy Guidelines

If you are having problems with your school district's food allergy policies, go to this link for fantastic downloads of sample 504 Plans, Constructive Classroom and Non-Food Reward Ideas, Emergency Action Plans, and more. Every school district in the nation should take a more proactive approach in developing guidelines in order to protect food-allergic children and provide maximum inclusion within their classrooms.
www.isbe.net/nutrition/htmls/food_allergy_guidelines.htm

Index